THE LIFE OF 'KIWI' BRIAN

The amazing success story of
Brian 'Kiwi' Adamson
Self-made millionaire

Gambler Playboy
World Traveller

By

David St John

First published by DSJP
(Previously published as The Life of Brian!)

©David St John 2020

COPYRIGHT

All rights reserved. No part of this publication may be reproduced, stored in a retrieval system, or transmitted in any form or by any means, electronic, electrostatic, recording, magnetic tape, mechanical, photocopying or otherwise, without prior permission in writing from the publishers. The publishers make no representation, express or implied, with regard to the accuracy of the information contained within this publication and cannot accept any responsibility in law for any errors or omissions.

The publishers have made every reasonable effort to trace the copyright owners of any image contained in this book. In the event of any omission, the publishers will be pleased to hear from anyone who has not been appropriately acknowledged, and to make a correction in any further reprints and publications. Many photographs throughout this book are personal photographs supplied by Brian Adamson. Some photographs are also copyrighted to the author, with this paperback containing B&W images in line with standard printing costs. Many of these same photographs can be viewed in the original colour as copied from the originals, should the reader wish to purchase the digital e-book version of this same publication.

The right of David St John to be identified as author of this Work has been asserted by him in accordance with sections 77 and 78 of the Copyright, Designs and Patent Act 1988.

CONTENTS

IN THE BEGINNING

COSTA DEL KIWI!

CHAPTERS:
1. BIRTH OF A LEGEND
2. NATURAL BORN FIGHTER
3. SURVIVOR
4. HELLO SAILOR!
5. THE GAMBLER
6. SOUTHAMPTON
7. KING OF CLUBS
8. THE SILHOUETTE CLUB
9. THE GOLDEN YEARS
10. BACK TO SEA –WITH A DIFFERENCE!
11. THE SEVENTIES
12. SEVENTIES SCANDAL!
13. THE EIGHTIES
14. THE EIGHTIES UPS AND DOWNS
15. END OF AN ERA
16. CARRY ON UP THE MED!
17. NEW SILHOUETTE IN THE SUN
18. THE NAUGHTY NINETIES
19. PHUKET!
20. MARBELLA
21. MISCELLANEOUS MEMORIES
22. EPILOGUE
23. FAMOUS NAMES AND PLACES

IN THE BEGINNING.....

This is an amazing story of a handsome young New Zealand lad, who landed in England back in the late Fifties. Brian 'Kiwi' Adamson had a vision, imagination with dreams that really did come true. In a very short time, he became a self-made millionaire playboy, gambler and world traveller, bedding over 2,000 gorgeous ladies along the way! Determined to make a success of his life - and he did it! It must all be seen in context with the decades that went before us, as life was very different back then!

His favourite phrase during his wild years: "Why buy a book, when you can join a library?" Amusingly, his randy bachelor status was put on hold for a short period whilst in his early fifties, marrying a beautiful young lady, some thirty years his junior. Sadly, this union only lasted a couple of years, before returning to his old 'sexploits', setting off for more journeys around the globe.

This book tells of his rollercoaster years, opening a small club/casino that soon became one of the finest venues in the South. Kiwi's famous Silhouette nightspot is still fondly remembered by the lucky generation that flocked to the club for the best night out for miles around. It was the first Southampton nightclub to open after the war, as well as being the 9th casino in the UK to obtain a gaming licence when new restrictions were introduced. It was also the longest-running nightclub under the same ownership over three decades, providing the best night out for miles around.

After nearly thirty successful years, Brian decided to sell up in order to become even more of a world traveller, visiting many of the great cities and the top casinos in Las Vegas etc. Recent times saw him flitting between Spain, Thailand and Australia, buying and selling luxurious properties, before winding it all down after a hectic lifetime that few of us could imagine.

Now in his mid-Eighties, he has settled in the jet-set suburb of Puerto Banus, rubbing shoulders with fellow millionaires, who flock to Marbella on the Costa del Sol. Sun, sea, sand and sex are the main ingredients of this beautiful part of Spain, which mirror this great character's past, although advancing years have naturally diminished Kiwi's capers. However, he still has a twinkle in his eye, constantly scanning the beautiful girls of all ages, as they parade through the swish harbour. His gift of the gab is still working well, often chatting up the pretty ladies who cross his path on his daily strolls around the resort, albeit he is still on crutches for now. This followed an unfortunate freak accident, when falling out of a car in late 2017, breaking his hip as well as causing some nerve damage. As you will learn later in the early chapters, Brian was – and still is a fighter, determined to carry on as best as he can despite this setback

Attitudes have changed dramatically in recent times, with the over-used 'sexist' label being attached to any tales such as you will read in this book. We live in a PC-driven society these days, but one must not forget that Brian's 'escapades' were all part of the 'permissive society' that exploded in the Swinging Sixties as the young generation threw off the shackles of their parents' way of life. Please bear this in mind as you learn about the erotic side of this playboy's life, in between the impressive business profile that grew across the early years of his younger days, along with the big gambles in his life.

You must put any prejudices aside, as the main period of this book centres on the Swinging Sixties, where anything - and everything went, as they said back then. You may already have preconceived thoughts on a story like this, labelling this libidinous lothario's past life as 'sexist'. Nothing could be further from the truth, as Brian Adamson never had the need to force himself on any of the many women across his rampant years. The sex was always consensual, and quite easy to understand the attraction of a good-looking millionaire club owner, who could charm the birds out of the trees. More to the point, he charmed many 'birds' straight into his bed, with mutual satisfaction to the fore.

We open this story in July 2019, when the author was invited out to meet up with the legend that is Brian 'Kiwi' Adamson – Playboy, Gambler and World Traveller extraordinaire!

Brian Adamson 2019

My personal link to this great character had surfaced back in 2011, when I received a surprise e-mail from the man himself. He had stumbled across my own website, containing a massive wealth of information on the Sixties music scene around my birthplace of Southampton. Brian had landed in the town during the 1950s as one of thousands of Merchant Navy crew members, immediately falling in love with the place. Despite only being in his late Twenties, with a few hundred pounds in his pocket, Kiwi went about fulfilling his burning ambition to open up a nightclub, which soon developed into one of the most popular venues in the South of England. He recognised many of the names and places that I have written about over recent years, so then sent me some of his own rare collection of photos plus his own self-penned account of his incredible life. I uploaded a dedicated webpage, including a copy of a great article that was published in the Southern Echo back in 2011. Ex-Sotonian Ash Bolton has lived in the Marbella area for some years, being a well-established freelance journalist, writing for the local Spanish press such as *'El Sur'* and other outlets.

He has kindly given permission to reproduce the heading, showing this photo of a very relaxed Brian Adamson, along with the text that outlines much of his life. Some while after appreciating my sharing some of his story, Brian suggested that I might with to undertake the task of getting a book published as there was much more he has to share when looking back over many years. I have written it all in a chronological order from his early family life in New Zealand, through his teenage years during which he first had a taste of publicity that inspired his later years. Much of the story is centred on Southampton, from Kiwi's rapid rise to top nightclub owner across the Sixties to the late Eighties. The later years saw him enjoying the delights of Thailand before settling in Marbella which provides him with the lifestyle that suits him perfectly.

FEATURE

> He turned £300 into £3m... now former Hampshire resident Brian Adamson is planning to publish his life story. ASH BOLTON catches up with him at his luxury apartment in the Spanish resort of Marbella

From dishwasher to multi-millionaire

Courtesy © Southampton Echo/Ash Bolton

ROM DISHWASHER TO MULTI-MILLIONAIRE
Published 2011

He turned £300 into £3m . . . now former Hampshire resident Brian Adamson is planning to publish his life story. ASH BOLTON catches up with him at his luxury apartment in the Spanish resort of Marbella

To say former Southampton nightclub owner Brian Adamson has led an interesting life is a bit of an understatement. Among his claims to fame are gambling with Sinatra in Las Vegas, owning one of the most luxurious nightclubs outside London and losing $240,000 during a drink-fuelled gambling session with a Pakistani arms dealer. Now the 77-year-old, who has spent the past 22 years living in Marbella, is in the process of getting his life story published to help inspire young people to follow their dreams. Brian's story began when he became New Zealand's feather-weight boxing champion at the age of 15, an achievement that gave him a sense of wanderlust. Brian said: "I didn't want to get cauliflower ears so I gave it up. But boxing gave me this travel bug. "I remember putting a pin in the map of all the countries and capitals in the world that I wanted to go to in life and apart from Berlin, I've done the lot."

At 18 he set off for the UK to become a radio operator at the air training school at Hamble. But after lasting just three months due to too many nights out partying in Southampton, he joined the Merchant Navy. During this stage of his flamboyant career he worked as a dishwasher on the Queen Mary, a ship he was later to rejoin as a millionaire passenger on its final voyage. While at sea, Brian used his earnings to buy furniture overseas before storing it away in a garage. When he returned to Southampton in 1960 he took out a lease on a warehouse for £6 a week on St Michael's Square. He gambled his £300 savings on expanding three rooms over an off-licence to create the Flamingo Club. But it seems lady luck dealt him a winning hand as he became one of the richest men in the city when he renamed it The Silhouette Club in 1962. It was one of Southampton's first night clubs since the war and only the ninth casino in Britain to be issued with a gambling licence when it was legalised in 1968. He said: "I always wanted to be my own boss and I thought what should I open, a restaurant or a club? "I thought there are too many restaurants in Southampton and only two clubs. I was my own barman, doorman and cleaner and I paid a girl to come in on Friday and Saturday nights to help me. "If I couldn't afford it I wouldn't buy it until I had the cash. The liquor suppliers would do a sale or return so I never had to pay out for drinks I didn't sell. "As I made money I ploughed it back into the bar. I had a one-arm bandit which used to make a lot of money and I kept the rough guys out as I was pretty tough. It just went from strength to strength."

During this time he also opened a coffee shop called Down Under and an eatery called Kiwi Restaurant in the city, which he later incorporated into The Silhouette Club. Brian's nightclub started building a reputation for itself after troops from two American aircraft carriers and Miss UK made appearances at the business. Brian was the first person to cross Southampton's iconic Itchen Bridge when it opened on June 1 1977. Clutching a glass of champagne, the media savvy millionaire crossed the bridge in an 18th-century horse drawn landau with his girlfriend at the time in view of the local media. Between 1962 and 1983 Brian's gambling caught the attention of several large casinos who invited him on all expenses paid trips to gamble his new found fortune. During these hedonistic years he met an assortment of celebrities including Burt Reynolds, Muhammad Ali, Tom Selleck, Frank Sinatra, George Best and Shirley Bassey.

He said: "The casino reps invited me to play and paid all my expenses including air fares, luxury suites and limousines. And for that they expected me to gamble in high figures. One time they sent me an invitation to fly by Concorde to a casino in Atlantic City. I told them I've already been on Concorde so I arrived on the Queen Elizabeth. They paid for everything. I was then picked up by helicopter on arrival at New York and flown to Atlantic City." He added that the most he ever won in one sitting was $84,000 at the world's most famous casino, Caesar's Palace in Las Vegas. But he normally won between $25,000 and $45,000. "One cardinal gambling sin that I once broke was to drink and chase with another gambler who was the arms buyer for Pakistan. We were at a Casino called the Desert Inn in Las Vegas.

"The first three days I was there I was $60,000 up and on the fourth day I was $240,000 down. We were playing Baccarat and betting $10,000 on the turn of a card. "But I didn't get upset. I just took it as part of life. I was winning eight out of ten times on average." It was around this time that the high roller made what he describes as the biggest regret of his life by turning down an invitation to a party at Hugh Hefner's Playboy Mansion. "I was sitting next to the director of a

TV show on a flight from London to Los Angeles. He said would I like to go to Hugh Hefner's mansion. My regret was that I was too eager to get to the gaming tables in Las Vegas. When I phoned him a few days later he was too busy to take my call. I've been kicking myself ever since. It would have been a great night", he added mournfully.

In 1987 he sold the business to Southampton based company Leading Leisure for £3m. But months later the Silhouette was wrecked by fire and he ended up losing £1m after the company went bust. He then famously burnt his useless shares in front of local TV crews outside the charred remains of the nightclub he used to own. It was at this stage that he decided to move to the Costa del Sol. He said: "I had had enough after 27 years so I decided to finish and get out. I already had a boat moored here called "No Harassment." Brian then opened a restaurant and piano bar in Puerto Banús called The Silhouette where he said a number of gangsters and celebrities drank. But the business only lasted two years due to what he called "bad management". It then re-opened on three occasions as a lap dancing club and is now being rented out as a bar playing live music.

Nowadays the dad of two spends his time living between properties he owns in Thailand and Marbella. Sitting in his luxury apartment he chuckles that he has "led the life of three" and is now looking to find a woman to settle down with. But as for his book, which is currently in need of a ghost writer, he said: "I want to let young people know that you just need to take initiatives to be prosperous. It can be done. To achieve you must be prepared to work long hours and not cheat people.

"My father always told me that you can always get money but if you lose your reputation it goes with you to the grave." As for his gambling days he added: "I still go to the local casino but in a few months I'm thinking of doing a trip back to Las Vegas for old time's sake."

Ash Bolton 2011

COSTA DEL KIWI!

David St John writes:

Like many 'Baby Boomers' born just after the war, my early years were a great period of my life, growing up in one of the finest towns in England. Southampton was an exciting place to be, throughout the Sixties, especially for this young lad, having left school in 1964, so just in time to enjoy the nightlife around the busy port. My teenage years were taken up with 'day' jobs, whereas my evenings saw me singing with various local pop groups, in between pub visits with my pals.

Everybody knew of the Silhouette club, situated in an alleyway next to St Michael's Church, in the oldest part of the town, just a stone's throw from the Docks. The original Flamingo nightclub had opened its doors in 1960 under the guidance of a bright young New Zealander, who had taken advantage of his shore leaves on previous visits as a merchant seaman, in order to find some roots. He fell in love with the area and the people – especially the local ladies, who fell for his looks and smooth-talking talents. His initial stay was intended to boost his naval capabilities, with a short-lived training course as a maritime radio operator in nearby Hamble. The distractions of the opposite sex, combined with lack of money led to his dropping out of his studies to take up a boring temporary job, as a stop-gap before fulfilling his main ambition to open up his own business.

By 1963, the renamed venue was well established, as well as everybody knowing of its owner Brian 'Kiwi' Adamson, one of the most well-known local characters of all time. Sadly, I never frequented the club, although several of my local musician pals and DJs were booked there throughout the years. By 1972, I had left Southampton, to pursue my new way of life as a professional comedy entertainer. In recent years, I had set up a personal website, initially to promote myself, then expanding it to include a massive wealth of web-pages, highlighting the Hampshire music scene of the early years. With the advent of the web, boosted by social media, I was receiving messages from all over the world, as people searched on relevant names and places, leading them straight to me. A surprise e-mail popped up in 2011, from Brian Adamson, who was now settled in Marbella, but still retaining a love of Southampton, where his own life had really taken off. We exchanged some great messages and phone calls, along with him posting some amazing photos that highlighted a part of his life, plus his own potted autobiography. Although in his late Seventies by then, Brian had encompassed technology to a small degree, leading to a basic working knowledge on a PC.

I was able to write up a dedicated webpage, that soon became highly visited, with an increasing number of 'hits', due to Kiwi and his Silhouette Club being very well known from those who remembered the venue. He liked my style of writing, which led to him asking if I would undertake the task of publishing his biography. Sadly, due to other commitments, I was not able to accommodate this request at that time. Late 2017 gave me the opportunity with more free time to accept a deal, leading to Brian's kind offer to invite me over to Marbella for a few days. This was for a meet-up, interview plus the chance to look through his collection of photo albums and press cuttings over the last sixty odd years. My flight was booked, but cancelled at the last minute, due to an accident that hospitalised Brian for a few months, leading to a long period of mobility issues.

Undeterred, I was able to write up most of this book through 2018, as we exchanged more emails, phone calls along with Brian sending more photos, newspaper cuttings etc. These helped to elaborate on his various escapades, which now form this biography – it would make for a good film script! By the summer of 2019, Kiwi felt fit enough to invite me over to his new apartment in Puerto Banus, which was my first ever visit to Spain. My flight from Birmingham landed at Malaga airport, with a pleasant 45 minute bus trip to Marbella, followed by a short taxi ride to central Puerto Banus. Leaving the taxi, I saw Kiwi across the road, standing by the luxury apartment block, smiling and waving one of his crutches in the air!

We hugged, like old pals having known each other for some while, albeit at a distance, before going through the concierge desk, leading to the lift that whisked us up to his front door, leading to his new bachelor pad. His large fully equipped spacious apartment, recently purchased from a Russian millionaire, leads to an enclosed sun-drenched balcony, overlooking the beautiful square of Plaza de Antonio Banderas, named in honour of the locally-born Hollywood A-lister. To get to the nearby marina, one crosses the Avenue de Julio Iglesias, another big name from the Malaga area, with other lesser-known celebrities lending their names to other thoroughfares. We spent most of the afternoon, having a good chat about our respective years back in Southampton, as well as my being able to take notes from his albums, plus scanning some more rare personal photos. Despite the usual bouts of memory loss as we all get older, Brian's face lit up as he recalled many milestones in a lifetime of excess, with names, faces and places, many of which can be found in these very pages

Brian's classy apartment is perfectly situated, with all amenities within walking distance. The luxurious El Cortes Ingles department store lies just across the road – one of its largest outlets across Spain. There are banks, shops, cafes and everything to hand, with bars, boutiques and restaurants within the central area, so he is more than happy at relocating here after a lifetime of global travel. The residents also have exclusive use of the private gardens with swimming pool, surrounded by glorious foliage and palm trees.

It soon became obvious that Kiwi is also a fairly well-known character around the marina, as we went for a walk along the harbour road, known as 'the Golden Mile' passing by many of the massive 'superyachts' moored along the quay. Kiwi had his own yacht moored here, in which he had sailed from Southampton a few years before. Later on, you will certainly be amused at what happened on that remarkable journey as well as how the boat made local and national headlines, just after Brian sold it!

The King of Saudi Arabia, plus many of the world's wealthiest people have permanent moorings in this prime location, providing a glimpse of the other side of life for the tourists who throng to this slice of paradise. The adjacent parking spaces boast collections of Ferraris, Rolls Royces, Bentleys, Lamborghinis and many more luxury cars that complement the whole experience of this millionaires' playground. I visited Monte Carlo a few years ago, which was pretty impressive. Puerto Banus, although much smaller, is even more of a jaw-dropping experience, with a beautiful atmosphere and all year round sunshine – hence the Spanish name of La Costa del Sol.

We stopped to chat to various people on the way, followed by a superb meal at the very popular Picasso restaurant, but noticing the long queue outside, as diners waited for a place at this much sought-after establishment, named after another local celebrity. The head waiter ushered us straight in, much to the disdain of some of those waiting on the pavement, as another waiter led us to a good table. We were served immediately, as it became apparent that Kiwi was a regular customer, who was always fast-tracked whenever he popped by. I commented on this, causing him to laugh and quip "I don't do queues…"

He spends some of his time by reading books, watching television with many UK channels to keep him up to date with news and programmes 'back home'. In addition, he has daily walks, meeting up with many of his friends and business colleagues around the port. He also relies on Jane, a lovely Filipino lady who does a great job of looking after Kiwi, with cooking, household chores as well as making sure he takes the prescribed medication for his various health issues. Brian jokes *"It's like having a wife but without the sex!"* Brian also looks after himself fairly well, with a strong streak of independence which impresses everybody around him.

He also mentioned some special people, who have become good friends ever since he arrived in Marbella. They help to run his day to day affairs, including his personal physician - Doctor Victoria Chalon, assisted by her very competent secretary Nievisi. Victoria actually saved his life a while back, as you will later learn, so a special bond exists as you can well imagine. Brian's financial dealings are dealt with by another good friend in the shape of Joaquin Lopez Toro. He is a business manager at the Sabadell Sol Bank Puerto Banus, keeping a close watch on Brian's various business interests over a long period.

Other close friends include two of his lawyers – Roberto Sanchez, of the long-established Lawbird firm of solicitors, based in Marbella plus Jose Hinosa, with both of these top specialists taking care of any legal issues. Brian has never managed to learn much Spanish, but most Puerto Banusians speak English, so he rarely has any conversational problems. He loves the Spanish people who are very friendly and polite, even when approaching any road crossing, as the vehicles stop right away – unlike many countries where you take your life in your hands! Honesty prevails as well, as Kiwi mentioned his weekly visits to the casino, on Tuesdays and Fridays. On one such trip back by taxi, he inadvertently left 650 Euros on the back seat, when taking his money out to pay the driver who then drove off. Within minutes, the cabbie returned, much to Brian's relief and gratitude- this met with an extra big tip as you will have guessed.

2009 saw him take part in a national tournament, leading to the first place, fighting off tough opposition at the Casino Marbella. Not the biggest of pots that Kiwi is used to, but more than happy with the prestige plus 5,680 Euros!

RESULTADO TORNEOS NACIONALES

TORNEOS POKER IN, CASINO DE BARCELONA. 110€ FREEZEOUT. SEPTIEMBRE 2009.

Fecha	Lugar	Vencedores	Premio
14/09/09	Casino de Barcelona	Xavier Bonareu	4,400€
21/09/09	Casino de Barcelona	Arturo Espuny	4,590€

FRIDAY POKER FEVER. CASINO MARBELLA. SEPTIEMBRE.

Fecha	Lugar	Vencedores	Premio
04/09/09	Casino Marbella	Gary Collins	5,285€
11/09/09	Casino Marbella	Ernesto Jiménez "Grischuk"	5,200€
18/09/09	Casino Marbella	Bryan Adamson	5,680€

His brain and gambling instincts are still working well, with his regular jaunts to the club generally going his way. Kiwi takes part in the popular 'Texas Hold'em' tournament, which sees a number of poker players place their bets into the pot. Recent sessions have seen him walking away with a few first prizes, beating other players in the early rounds, before taking his place on the last table of the ten finalists. He recently made it to the final, sharing the pot with Rosa, another regular winner, so more than happy with the result!

Finalists- Ros and Kiwi

It is a fun night out, plus the chance to meet up with his many pals in the great surroundings, as well as enjoying a super meal at the top class restaurant. After a lifetime in the club and casino business, Brian knows a lot about the whole business, with the Casino Marbella being one of his most highly-rated establishments, where he really feels 'at home'. The friendly management and highly trained staff plus luxurious surroundings fit perfectly with the experience that is Puerto Banus.

Kiwi with a stack of high value chips!

Casino Marbella gaming tables

After a couple of wonderful days, it was reluctantly time for me to get back to the UK, having enjoyed the hospitality and company of this fascinating man. I asked him why he wanted to share his life story, but

I already knew the answer, as it would be a shame to lose such an incredible description of what he had achieved. Photos and newspaper clippings can often be lost or put into storage, so never seeing the light of day. This book contains many great memories from a fun-packed life, taken from Brian's photo albums. Including one of his favourite places, on a yacht, sailing around Lake Mead. All courtesy of Caesars Palace Las Vegas, part of the complimentary hospitality packages, offered to their best guests. What a life....

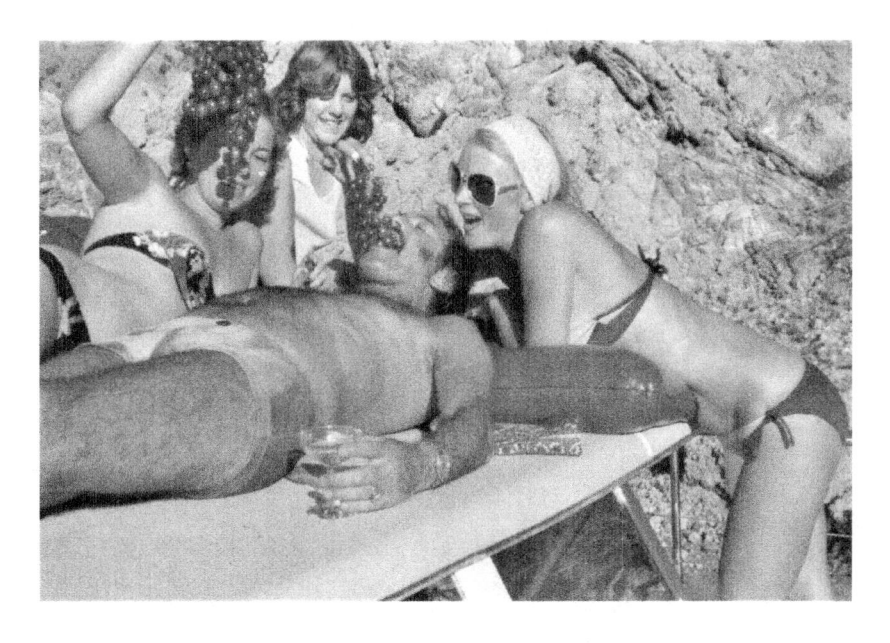

"Girls - peel me a grape!"

His collection of memorabilia contained in the many albums could have filled two books as part of his story, but it was decided to include as many relevant images as possible in this publication. The celebrity photographs bear testimony to how he mingled with so many stars of stage, screen, sport and music all over the world on his many travels. Many of these same people were fascinated by Brian's own life story, when they learned of his early years as an ambitious young entrepreneur back in New Zealand. Quite often, the rich and famous also come from humble beginnings, thus enabling Kiwi to talk to them on the same level.

They also suggested that "You should write a book about it all!" as they laughed at some of antics that he shared with them in private conversations. It may have taken a long time to see it all in print, but better late than never.

Brian also commented that perhaps another young man - or woman might be inspired to take a chance in life, as success usually breeds success. Some of us can make our own luck. Time now to go back to where it all began…..

Adamson Family Crest

Chapter 1 BIRTH OF A LEGEND

The Thirties was a decade that witnessed major changes across the world, as Great Britain was recovering from the ravages of the Great War of 1914/1918, having lost millions of young lives as well as becoming nearly bankrupt. The sun had already set on the Empire that saw Queen Victoria's age of invention and discovery overshadowed by global conflict, but the Commonwealth still survived to some degree. America was also gripped by the great Depression, following the Wall Street Crash of 1929, resulting in many countries being affected by the problems of the two main world players. Stock markets have always been based on a form of gambling, so there is a tenuous link within this story.

Australia and New Zealand have both seen mass immigration over the previous centuries, as many Europeans upped sticks to sail away to a new life Down Under. Both of these Antipodean countries had also suffered the losses of many of their brave armies during WW1, notably the ANZAC losses at Gallipoli, as the brave troops were cut down by the Turkish forces in 1915. Whilst many new settlers chose to land on Australian shores, with its exciting opportunities of employment and a life in the sun, many more sailed even further to one of the most scenic countries on earth.

The indigenous Maori people had already staked their own claims on this new land some 800 years before, followed by the new wave of immigrants in recent times. New Zealand is a sparsely-populated country of nearly five million being mainly spread across the North and South Island, boasting spectacular greenery, mountains, lakes, as well as having a temperate climate. Its main exports have been based on the sheep trade, as well as agriculture and other commodities.

Upper Hutt was then a small town (now a city) around 20 miles from the capital of Wellington, on North Island with a current population of some 40,000, but its main colonisation only started back in the 1920s as many city people left the busy capital to seek a quieter kind of life in wonderful surroundings built up around its main river area. One of its most successful inhabitants was born on the 24th April 1934, and christened Brian Selwyn Adamson, the latest addition to the family of two older brothers. His star sign is Taurus and the characteristics certainly ring true, if you follow the fascinating study of astrology. This is one description that will make you smile as you read of the exploits of this new Kiwi baby!

"Taurus, the second sign of the zodiac, is all about reward. Unlike the Aries love of the game, Taurus loves the rewards of the game. Think physical pleasures and material goods, for those born under this sign revel in delicious excess. They are also a tactile lot, enjoying a tender, even sensual, touch." Says it all……

Former Adamson family home- 24 McParland Street Upper Hutt (1990)

New Zealanders Charlie and Elizabeth Adamson were already blessed with two sons, before the new addition came along who was christened Brian – all fairly traditional family set-ups in that era, but the new baby would certainly not conform to the way of life that was often mapped out for any youngster. Despite the hardships of the time, Brian had a very happy childhood, albeit at the bottom of the pecking order, until a young sister came along shortly after.

Cheeky charmer – aged 3

Brian's early years in this rural community saw him helping out with the family chores, with agriculture providing food and income for many small town people, as self-providing was the order of the day. The luxury of spending hard-earned money in local shops was a long way off for most of the Upper Hutters, but everybody seemed to manage. Education was also a priority, as all parents have aspirations for their offspring, but aware that they need to find their own feet in the years ahead. Brian's school years were somewhat of a disappointment, as his academic prowess never had a chance to develop, although there was a canny brain inside that young head, which would be put to great use in adult life. This young Kiwi may not have been a star pupil, but he was developing a cheeky character and a smooth way with words.

His good looks were also starting to become even more attractive to the opposite sex in the school yard and the neighbourhood, as the young girls flocked around him – a sign of things to come. Young Brian was intelligent, but let his mind drift out of the boring classroom window as he pondered his future as we all do at that age, knowing that a much more exciting life was on the horizon. Movies and magazines showed a completely different lifestyle, offering escapism from a dreary existence, which is what was about to happen to this young daydreamer within a few short years ahead. He would become part of this gilded existence that he had read about, but made it a reality.

Teenage dream boy – Mom's face says it all

Chapter 2 NATURAL BORN FIGHTER

By the age of twelve, Brian had 'lost his cherry' with a pretty young blonde in a dark alleyway, thus setting the template of what lay ahead. He was also quite athletic and a love of sports overshadowed his academic under-achievements, which is a common thread with many of the younger generation. Schoolboy scraps were quite common and Brian was no stranger to several punch-ups in the playground, or out of the school area. Much of the aggro seemed to be down to his handsome features that were attracting the females all around him, so the seeds of jealousy amongst other lads were germinating, leading to scuffles all over the place. His prowess at rugby and football also attracted attention, which also racked up the envy levels of many schoolmates, but he always came out top in any altercation.

On one of many occasions, a few verbal childish insults had escalated to yet another challenge of fisticuffs on a patch of dusty bare ground near the main High Street shops. Away from the prying eyes in the school yard, Brian and his latest opponent squared up to each other, as a small crowd of excited young onlookers gathered round in eager anticipation. It provided some entertainment as there wasn't much to do in those days for the youngsters, and this latest flurry would result in a positive outcome for 'Basher Brian' as he was christened in these early years. The punches flew as the two protagonists ducked and dived, with the 'ringside' onlookers shouting encouragement to whichever scrapper was their mate. The noise soon attracted attention from the passers-by, as well as some of the nearby shopkeepers who came out to see what the fuss was all about.

One of the men ran across the street, pushing his way through the young crowd, grabbing the two fighters by the scruff of the neck, their arms still flailing wildly as they tried to get a late punch in. The man then shooed everybody away, dragging the two lads back to his shop, as they wiped traces of blood off their grubby faces plus cleaning the dust away from their clothes. Tempers soon cooled, with reluctant handshakes, aided by a couple of ice creams from the shop, plus a few words from the unexpected referee who had stopped the fight in the early rounds. This struck a chord with Brian, seemingly being rewarded for a juvenile boxing fight as he knew he was good with his fists if provoked. He was not a hot-headed child and never labelled as a bully around the community, so these early signs paved way for an important change in his life.

As it happened, Charlie Adamson helped out at the local boxing club and whilst sharing a cold beer with owner Roy McCrae, he was taken aback when being told that his son had some potential in the noble art. It transpired that the very same shopkeeper who rushed in to stop the brawl was the very same gym owner, and he had held back for a short while, observing the slim lad who was ducking and diving with some style in his footwork, as well as landing some well-aimed blows to his opponent. The intervention certainly came as a reprieve for the other boy, who was no match for this plucky youth, with no towel to be thrown into the ring. Derek suggested that this potential tearaway would be well suited to undertake some training as he had a good temperament, attitude and a natural talent.

Charlie went home and had a chat with Elizabeth, with this latest news that made some sense as it might serve as an opportunity, giving Brian a sense of purpose as well as a way to instil some discipline. Controlled boxing has always offered many a young man a way to escape from bad surroundings, unsatisfactory family life or in the absence of any reasonable academic levels that might hinder a life ahead. His home life was very happy, and his parents and family were naturally keen for their lad do well in the years that followed, so encouraged him in whatever he wanted to do.

Brian and his father were invited along to take a look at the set-up, being the first time that he had ever stepped inside such a club. He was immediately impressed, as he watched amateur boxers of all ages sparring away, knowing deep inside that he could whip a few asses right away! The walls were plastered with certificates and shelves stacked with trophies, ribbons and other artefacts that highlighted the

Upper Hutt Boxing Club's standing, as it regularly outshone the opposition from other boxing clubs in the area. The smell of old leather, sweat and embrocation hung in the air, giving it all a surreal atmosphere that appealed to the novice fighter who showed an immediate interest, much to the delight of the owner who was pretty astute at recognising untapped talent. This new path in life would later manifest itself in the years to come as he fought his way up in the word, and being tough-but fair, certainly helped Brian to take on many battles and challenges over the next few decades.

Champion in the making

The small joining fee was paid, as the newest young member got stuck into the rigorous early training schedules as well as enjoying a new circle of mates who shared the same interest. His skinny, but tough body carved out a role as a featherweight, but he was often paired up with older tougher adolescents, many of whom helped out with physical work in the surrounding fields of this agricultural community. However, brains, and not brawn, kicked in as Brian's natural skill and determination to win soon gained momentum, resulting in the proud Adamson household finding room for the never ending succession of his own trophies, plaques, ribbons and much more proof of how well he was progressing. Their son was the talk of the town over the next three years, with local press reports that gave Brian a sense of pride, as well as enhancing his profile as a ladies' man.

Brian soon became aware of the power of publicity, as his status was being boosted by the media, and he made good use of this in his later life, when making sure that the local press were made aware of anything that grabbed headlines. Self-publicity is a talent, with many an insignificant story being picked up by the larger media outlets that feed on anything that can be utilised for their own purposes. This soon became apparent to Brian as his fame was spreading outwards. Thanks to the internet, one can actually read up on newspaper archives, due to those who take the trouble to share slices of modern history, and here is one of many local cuttings from the Upper Hutt Leader (December 1949) via the City Library pages.

"Brian Adamson and Ronny Fallpon, both of Heretaunga gym put on a thrilling three round contest at the recent tournament held in Wellington to aid the Blind Childrens' fund. After a keenly contested bout in which both boys boxed brilliantly, Adamson received the referee's decision. This was the last bout of the season for these two boys. They both have had a successful year and have engaged in contests with the best boys in their division in New Zealand"

Any sports-person has a yearning to make a mark in his or her chosen path, with the late Forties and Fifties seeing the likes of Joe

Louis, Sugar Ray Robinson, Jake La Motta, Rocky Marciano and many more boxing idols that inspired many a young boxer, but no featherweights were recognised. Within a few years, Brian would be rubbing shoulders with the likes of Mohammed Ali, Mike Tyson and a whole host of celebrities as he was a regular ringside VIP spectator in Las Vegas and elsewhere, as well as mixing with them on a social level. By the age of fifteen, New Zealand had a new light featherweight champion, with Brian often surrounded by adoring female fans as he smiled into many a camera lens.

His new found fame also instilled a love of travel, as he made many journeys by road and rail in new parts, as well as enjoying the luxury of hotel stays. What a great way to escape a small town, as the world was a big place, waiting to be discovered and this was all cultivating a wanderlust plus another kind of lust in this handsome young man. In years to come, this tough Kiwi certainly combined the two words of wander and lust!

Brian on the right

This kid is a winner!

Teenage Brian

Boxing was a short period in this youngster's life, but great fun as it lasted. He knew that it could be a hard way to make a living, with many risks of injury plus many other factors that made him think more about what the future held for him. An imminent train journey was another incident that spurred Brian on to the next stage of an eventful life, as it made him realise how short this very life could be.

Chapter 3 SURVIVOR

Upper Hutt was an idyllic town to grow up in, as befits one of the most beautiful countries in the world with spectacular scenery and a gentle way of life, but this teenager was on the verge of flying the nest. With his new found love of travel, thanks to his sporting achievements, Brian took a keen interest in reading travel books. The more he read – the more he longed to visit many of the fascinating places all over the big wide world outside of his small community. Little did he realise how soon these dreams would come true within the space of a few years.

On one of his visits to the local newsagent, he purchased a large map of the world which then played a pivotal part in this adventurer's ideas. Brian pinned it on his bedroom wall, gazing lovingly at so many countries and cities that he had read about, as well as forming part of his dreams, some of which stayed in his head as he woke up the next day. He also realised the many hurdles that he would have to overcome, with his dream of becoming a world traveller, from the financial angle as well as a game plan of whatever employment he might consider.

Red coloured pins were placed on the number one goals that buzzed around his head, with the blue colours relegated to second choices and backups. The yellow ones served as spares, but little did he realise that over the next few years, he would have fulfilled this teenage dream as he managed to clock up a few million miles, pursuing money, interests and many women along the way.

Australia was the nearest major location, being some 2,000 miles to the north, with its expanding major cities and an exciting way of life that Brian had read about, although being similar in many ways. Air travel was in its infancy back in the Fifties, so way out of reach for most people, with travel by sea being the main route, but not viable for young pockets. Like many school-kids, playing truant was often a way to escape the drudgery of boring lessons, with this fifteen year old being no exception during his final years of education. One of his favourite getaways was to catch a train into the capital city of Wellington that sits on the lower stretch of North Island, some twenty miles from home. A cheap ticket saw Brian enjoying the scenic route down from the greenery of the countryside, then passing alongside the sea area into the harbour before alighting from the train to explore the hustle and bustle of this vibrant city.

He was always looking over his shoulder in case someone recognised a lone teenage traveller, or if anyone queried his absence from a school or college, but he looked confident with an air of a much more mature young man. Many a sunny carefree day was spent wandering around the shops, parks and other interesting places before catching the afternoon train back to Upper Hutt, with the time neatly fitting his journey back to the unsuspecting household.

The post-war New Zealand train infrastructure, as in many countries across the world, was naturally run down, with poor levels of maintenance and cost-cutting activities that put many lives in peril. However, there has always been another aspect of any tragedy that is often due to human error, negligence and apathy. One such event took place in June of 1949 when Brian boarded his usual local 10-30am train, that would take him off on yet another day of walking around, enjoying the sights and sounds of the city. He was fascinated by people and loved body-watching as he just sat gazing at the passers-by, wondering who they were and what they were doing in their lives.

As per normal, he chose a seat away from other passengers, still keeping a low profile on this particular weekday when he should have been studying at school. This off-peak train was fairly empty at that time of day, as Brian found a solitary seat in the front carriage, next to the window to enjoy the scenic ride as a great bonus to another 'bunking off' as we say in the UK.

The southbound train was travelling quite fast as it approached the outskirts of Wellington, passing alongside the busy harbour to the left side of the tracks, and as it approached the stop at Ngauranga station, little did anyone expect the tragedy that was unfolding. As the train slowed down, the driver was alarmed to see that a railway service crane was on the opposite northbound track, but the large jib had somehow come loose and had swivelled around to lie right across the southbound track in the path of the massive locomotive. The driver and cabin crew threw themselves across the floor as the heavy arm smashed into the windscreen, carrying on down the side of the carriages, ripping the sides away like a giant can opener within a few seconds.

There had been an almighty bang with the sound of screeching brakes and a burning smell from the undercarriage, as the whole line of carriages nearly tilted right over on its side, but the platform prevented this from happening. Screams filled the air, as the lucky ones made their way out of the smoking debris or tried to help those who had been sitting on that fateful side. Within minutes, the emergency services reached the spot, making frantic efforts to attend to the unfortunate travellers, treating the injured where they lay.

Other survivors were transported to nearby hospitals, clinics and doctors' surgeries, depending on the severity of their condition. Early reports indicated the loss of three lives, with many more injuries, some of which would result in long term hospital care, not forgetting the mental scars that remained for many years in the future.

Back home, in the Adamson home, it was just a normal quiet day as Elizabeth went about her daily chores, when a neighbour rushed in to tell her about the news reports. Brian's name had been mentioned along with more familiar locals, who had been on that very train, and one can only imagine the panic as everybody kept tuned to the radio as more updates came in. The police phone lines were jammed for hours as desperate relatives and friends called to check on the names as they were identified. Quite different to today, when instant rolling news from all over the world keeps us up to date by the minute, so it must have been a very difficult time for the town on that fateful morning.

Brian had escaped death by a whisker, soon recovering from the shock, although his main worry was that he was due to take part in an important boxing match in a few days, as part of the prestigious Heretaunga Club team. He was checked over by a doctor, who allowed him to be transported back to a very relieved family by taxi, boasting a two-way radio – quite a novelty for that time! Brian was interviewed on the day after this near miss, with this quote from the Upper Hutt Leader:

"The first I knew that I was thrown across the carriage. I scrambled to my feet and found the door jammed, so when the train finally stopped I stepped where the side of the carriage should have been. I think my cap and overcoat saved me from the flying glass and splinters. I thought we had hit another train, but my main worry was to get out"

Apart from his concern over his forthcoming boxing match, he was also worried what his parents might say to him, as they had no idea that an empty desk at school that day indicated yet another unauthorised absence. His fears were instantly resolved, as no punishment was meted out, apart from being sent to bed to rest for a few days, but interrupted by visitors who wanted to know all about his brush with the Grim Reaper. Inwardly, Brian was quite chuffed with the attention and more press reports, in addition to his ever increasing sporting wins, but he realised that Lady Luck had certainly been looking over him on that hot sunny day that could have been his last.

He was also thinking hard about his options for the immediate future, having doubts about his life of boxing and where it might take him. His lack of academic prowess narrowed the choices of imminent employment, and there was no way that this otherwise bright young man would consider a hard manual job out in the fields, or in some mind-numbing work in a factory or shop. He had a natural charm, handsome features as well as the ability to interact with people, and this came to fruition later in life, when he made his early start into the twilight world of nightclubs.

He was also more than aware that his very successful choice of sport had its drawbacks, in relation to poor prospects and, in the event of facing tougher challengers, he might fall victim to physical or even mental injury. The head is a target, with this face needing to be kept intact, as any good-looking lad wanted to keep it that way. Broken noses, split lips and cauliflower ears are not conducive to attracting the ladies, so Brian was on the verge of hanging up his gloves, with new ideas and dreams on the horizon.

He had also seen many older worn-out boxers that had obvious signs of brain deterioration, after constant batterings in the ring, and by now he preferred more bouts between the sheets as his hormones were running wild, encountering many more pretty girls through his mid-teens. Life is a gamble, and can sometimes be cut short by bad luck. It was time for this lad to try his hand on the next stage of an eventful life that very few us of could ever imagine. A local press article showed the result of the first carriage that felt the full force of the impact on that awful day, with the story still being talked about after so many years. Later on in this story, you will read about another couple of Kiwi's close shaves that made headlines around the world, so this early experience certainly showed that someone 'up there' was looking after him. Maybe guardian angels do exist, as this youngster seemed to have a charmed life ahead of him, part of which saw him charming a never ending succession of lovely ladies on his travels around the planet.

"Wreckage of the first carriage from which a 15 year old boy walked only slightly injured. The first window in this carriage was the only one intact along the whole side of the train"

Maybe that guardian angel was looking down on the lad, as he was sitting next to this very same window that escaped the massive damage. A few years later, he survived a major disaster in another part of the world, thus proving that this kid was a survivor.

Chapter 4 HELLO SAILOR!

Schooldays are the best days of your life, so the old saying goes, but in Brian's case the best day was the last day, as he left his Alma Mater for the last time, ready to face the next stage of his young life. Upper Hutt was only a relatively small town, and his discreet sexual conquests were mounting up, plus the fact that there were only a limited number of possible couplings in the immediate vicinity. This was the early Fifties and young girls were terrified of getting caught in the act, followed by the neighbourhood gossip that only affected the female of the species. Boys could get away with sexual philandering with relative impunity, and actually gain some kind of standing as a local stud. Boys also could not fall pregnant, which would be the ultimate shame and sinful behaviour that could see many a young girl whisked away for a few months 'holiday with relatives'.

The usual route of getting married, settling down with the same woman, then ending up in some dead-end job filled Brian's head with horror. There were regrets, as he had a warm loving family, feeling lucky to have had such a good upbringing, but his parents had always encouraged and supported him in whatever he chose to do. Brian was the perfect son, never bringing any trouble back home, so the wrench of his leaving did cause a few tears for a while.

Living near the sea is always a bonus in life, and the pull of the waters can always tug the heartstrings, wherever one ends up in the world. Wellington Harbour offered glimpses of beautiful ships, with the busy cargo traffic as well as the navy vessels that dropped anchor in the surrounding area. Brian was also aware that the merchant seamen seemed to have a good life, as they came ashore for short visits, with wedges of cash to spend on smart clothes, or in bars where they attracted the attention of very attractive girls. 'All the nice girls love a sailor' goes the old song, but the bad ones do as well, which prompted this randy teenager into applying to join up.

This photograph was taken on a beach near Wellington in the early Fifties, along with a budding young Italian actress by the name of Lisa Gastoni. She later found fame, with an amazing lifelong career in the movie industry and a steady success in the industry across many decades. In the background lies the sea, with ships that soon transported him across the world as his Odyssey continued.

Lisa Gastoni and Brian

After the usual preliminary training, in which he made more new friends, enjoying the banter that goes with a life at sea, Brian passed with flying colours as his new superiors were perceptive in knowing which recruits would make the grade. Many drop out when they experience sea-sickness for the first time, or simply just get homesick after extended trips away from the Motherland. Not every port is exciting, and some are downright depressing with nothing to do or see.

Brian was tough, having no problems in knuckling down to this new adventure that provided him with a free bunk, meals plus a reasonable wage that could be saved, as there was nothing to spend it on in the middle of the Seven Seas. However, hitting the lively ports gave the opportunity to let off steam and sexual energy that had built up whilst on the waves. This was all part of the larger vessels' way of life, as they travelled far and wide, but Brian's first experience was being placed in the galley of a fishing boat, which was very unfamiliar territory. Not domesticated in any way, having had all of his meals cooked by his mother as well as taking sandwiches to school, he faced the ovens, cooking ranges and utensils with a sense of foreboding. He had never even boiled an egg, let alone be trusted with helping the main cook with the preparation of meals for a hungry crew.

It didn't take long for the new boy to pick up the way in which it all worked, overcoming any disgruntled diner's comments with a few laughs as he dished out less than satisfactory culinary delights. His first experience at sea did not last as long as he had anticipated, due to an oversight that could have resulted in a major disaster, caused by his negligence. Brian forgot to fully switch off a gas burner, before leaving the galley for some while as the fumes filled the air, finding their way to a small pilot light on the other side of the cramped galley.

The explosion rocked the small boat, followed by a mad rush by the crew to extinguish the flames, allowing the acrid smoke to escape leaving a sorry spectacle of blackened bulkheads. The captain had no choice but to return to port, as any accident of this nature could cause the vessel to be un-seaworthy, so not the most auspicious start for the new sailor. He was also given leave, with a black mark on his records, hoping that this would not be the end of his new life on the briny.

Undeterred by his first experience, Brian's luck changed yet again, securing a position as deck hand on one of the many inter-island ferry boats out of Wellington Harbour. Working on these vessels, carrying passengers, mail and cargo, was far better than being stuck in a smelly galley, with Brian wallowing in healthy sea air as well as mixing with people of all ages, nationalities and even more pretty girls. Sailing between the main ports and smaller island harbours offered another tantalising taste of what lay outside the territorial waters of New Zealand.

Brian forged new shipmates as well as receiving good reports from the officers, who were very impressed with this lad who showed a natural aptitude. Sadly, this set of voyages did not work out as well as expected, due to a general negativity amongst the small crew as they had several issues with those above. Various degrees of disagreements over work conditions and pay led to a serious incident in which the lads downed tools, as well as neglecting important duties that threatened the safety levels at sea. It was then classified as a form of mutiny, which can never be tolerated in maritime law, as this could be very dangerous to everybody onboard.

With orders from the main shipping company, the hapless five mutineers were then offloaded at a small port on South Island then instantly dismissed, having to make their own way to wherever home was, or to seek employment elsewhere. Brian had no desire to strike, but the majority of his shipmates had taken drastic steps, so should not have been surprised at the outcome. He would have loved to have been part of the 'Mutiny On The Bounty' story, when the boatload of mutineers, led by Fletcher Christian, landed on Pitcairn Island in the Pacific Ocean back in 1789. These sex-starved sailors were greeted by loads of topless native girls who were fascinated by these friendly invaders, who soon settled down for some great times for years to come!

This problem also gave Brian more insights on how bosses and workers operated, as he watched, listened and learned how each side got on with each other. This all came into play later in life, as he built up his businesses with a keen eye on staff relations, plus the all-important loyalty and respect that makes for a successful environment. The insurgents were initially stranded far from their homes on the North Island, but were fortunate enough to have one of their number whose family home was on the South, so their hospitality provided a few of them with a place to crash for a while.

Money was scarce, before soon running out, which then saw the motley crew resort to stealing vegetables from nearby gardens and allotments during the hours of darkness. In days gone by, these mutineers might have met with some nasty retribution for this serious crime on the high seas. Flogging, prison or even ending up on the end of a rope, and left to rot as a warning to others!

In the meantime, the ship owners were playing for time, as they realised how good this particular crew had been, despite the severity of their reckless actions. Within a short time, approaches were made on both sides, and the (temporarily) jobless crew had no option but to offer their apologies as well as reluctantly agreeing to the new Draconian work schedules that they had first rebelled against. With tails between their sea legs, they all returned to the ferry boats, knuckling down to whatever their bosses dictated, albeit with a degree of sympathy from some of the management. Brian put this down to experience, returning home to Upper Hutt and a short taste of family life, before setting his sights far away from this part of the world. Once again, he took out his large map of the world, spread it across the bedspread, taking a red coloured drawing pin and sticking it firmly on a certain country that had been a long standing dream destination for some while. Fishing boats and ferries could never match the lure of the main oceans, and within a short while, Brian had applied for a place on an international cargo freighter. Little did he know that this wonderful destination would see the start of another turning in life, as he eventually settled there, taking a risk to set up a small business that exceeded his wildest dreams.

The vessel left the waters of the Southern Ocean, leading to the South Atlantic as it made its slow progress across thousands of miles over the next few weeks. Brian's first port of call saw him land in Belfast Northern Ireland, with a short stay as part of the cargo was unloaded thus giving him a taste of wandering around the city, plus a few beers in local pubs. This was a very different world, and within a short time, the ship sailed across the Irish Sea to dock at one of the most iconic ports that would soon be catapulted into global recognition. Liverpool was one of the busiest shipping cities, with the teenage Brian being overwhelmed by the docks traffic as hundreds of stevedores loaded and unloaded the cargo, with passenger ships jamming the harbour. A few miles away, the likes of John, Paul, George and Ringo were still at school, but all on the verge of making music, then eventually meeting up to lead the Mersey Beat sound that dominated the early Sixties and change the world forever.

A young Gerry Marsden was also practising guitar, singing the songs that were coming across from America, partly thanks to the Merchant Navy crews who were bringing back many early rock'n'roll discs that inspired these teenage Scousers. They were labelled 'The Cunard Yanks' who also brought back American comics, jeans, guitars and many more items that could be sold at a handsome profit. Later on, Brian was able to book Gerry and the Pacemakers plus many other top Sixties acts, whose hits are still heard all over the world today. He loved the accent and natural humour of this cosmopolitan city that produced many famous comedians over many years, as well as the exciting music that was first imported from the USA, then adapted to see the 'British Invasion' led by the Beatles and other top British pop groups in the early Sixties.

Our trainee 'world traveller' was sad to leave this exciting city, as the ship sailed away to start the 12,000 mile journey across the Atlantic on its way back home, via the Panama Canal, which was another amazing experience as the vessel slowly negotiated the narrow locks with inches on each side for the larger ships. Weeks at sea can be very boring, but Brian enjoyed the buzz of the whole scenario as he worked hard, in between enjoying the company of his shipmates as they talked for hours, or played cards to while away the time.

The mighty Pacific Ocean lay ahead, with another 7,500 miles to reach Wellington, so this young sea-dog was certainly clocking up the miles–the taste of things to come, but in a much different way of travelling. He arrived back home with a hefty wage packet, plus a warm homecoming from the proud Adamson family, friends and neighbours who wanted to hear about Upper Hutt's own 'Sinbad The Sailor' and his travels across the planet. Lots more 'sin' on the way.....

Brian was hardly one to sit around as he enjoyed working, so his next employment saw him undertaking a stevedore position at Wellington Harbour, but only for a short while as he saw the ships leave for more far-off destinations, wishing that he was on one of them. He had a message from the same freight company, asking if he might like to sign on again, being bound for England. It took a split second to agree, then he joined the ship but in a different crew position as a 'fireman' as stated in the Articles, although relegated in Merchant Navy terms, as a 'greaser' or 'grease monkey' so more hard graft was on the way. After another arduous few weeks at sea, the ship docked in Southampton, giving Brian the chance to discover more about this magnificent port city, in which he immediately felt 'at home' as he strolled around the town, which later achieved city status in 1964.

A few years before, the constant German bombing raids had flattened much of the docks and nearby buildings, being strategic targets to cause damage to the infrastructure of this main port. However, this did not seem to dampen the spirit of the Sotonians, who had always welcomed seafarers with open arms–and legs in many cases! Brian found them to very friendly, making new acquaintances that lasted for some time in the future as he chatted to people in local pubs and elsewhere. The whole country was getting back on its feet after the post-war austerity, with employment rising with the inevitable rise in finances, as well as the docks being full of ships, including the magnificent Cunard liners that saw the rich and famous disembark as they travelled on through the UK or Europe.

Towards the end of the decade, Brian undertook his last voyage as a member of a ship's crew, clocking up several thousand miles over the seas and oceans. This gave him an opportunity to visit Japan, which was another of his many red drawing pinned targets on his world map that he had pored over just a few years before setting sail to fulfil his dream. The British India Steam Navigation Company was a major shipping line that generally sailed between Southampton and Hong Kong.

The M.V. Nevasa was one of its main ships, which was also being used to pick up British troops and families from Japan, thus giving Brian a chance to visit a few amazing places within a few days as the ship was in port. She was one of the largest British troopship carriers and a fairly new ship, being built in 1955 on the River Clyde in Glasgow at some 20,000 tonnes. New style stabilisers offered the benefit of smooth sailing that made life much easier for everybody on board, and she had been kept busy with evacuating troops after the 1956 Suez crisis, plus the repatriation of troops across Asia, as the sun was setting on the old British Empire.

Brian was excited when the Nevasa docked at the major port of Kure, and even more excited when meeting up with a gorgeous Korean girl who offered to show him more sights in and out of the bedroom. The sex was amazing, and she soon taught this randy young sailor a thing or two that he had never imagined back in Upper Hutt. All part of life's rich tapestry that Brian was enjoying to the utmost, as would any young man at that time.

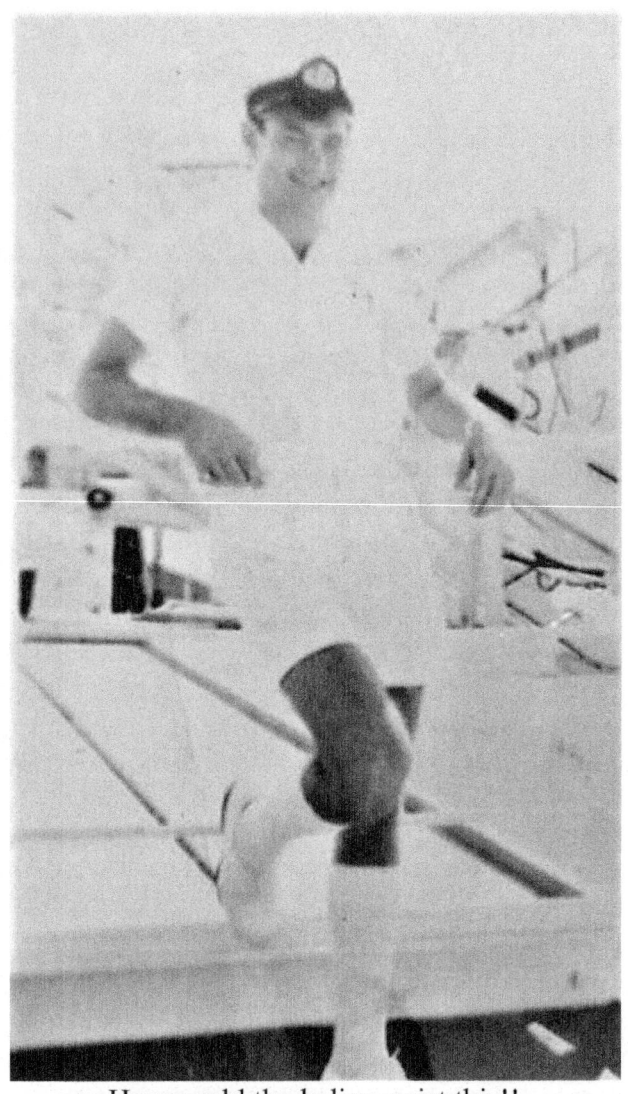

How could the ladies resist this!!

They spent some very happy days and hot steamy nights together, albeit with a sobering trip to the city of Hiroshima, whose museum displayed the horrors of warfare that had seen the city razed to the ground by US bombers, thus ending the war with Japan.

The second atomic bomb that was dropped on Nagasaki a few days later sealed the fate of the enemy country, as they had no choice but to surrender. Opinion has always been divided on this decision, as it saw terrible death and devastation on a massive scale, but it probably saved the lives of many prisoners of war in camps across Asia, as many Japanese wanted a fight to the death. One can only imagine the horrors that the weak starving survivors would have faced, so history has recorded this as a major turning point in modern times.

Brian and his new girl were shocked at the images and recorded memories of those fateful days in August 1945, as they wandered around the museum, leaving them with a feeling of deep sadness that had only taken place just a few years before this visit. He still recalls this eye-opening experience to this day, being just one of many memories that he has stored ever since, some good-some bad. The ship was a great experience too, as the itineraries were varied and he got on well with everybody onboard. The facilities were good, with top class food plus a well-stocked library that offered Brian the chance to read up on more world knowledge.

The spacious mess area/bar, universally known as 'The Pig & Whistle, also kept the crew occupied with board games with the inevitable pursuit of playing cards, giving this future entrepreneur a glimpse of how money could be made off the backs of unlucky gamblers. Many sailors had money to burn, after long trips at sea with little to spend it on, so a considerable amount could be won, or generally lost on these small card games.

Brian had become quite a good player after a good couple of years at sea, as well as reading up on the casinos all over the world and the tantalising glimpse of high rollers, with lifestyles to match. By now, he was running his own Crown and Anchor game - a sign of things to come! This was a very popular game played at sea by the Merchant and Royal Navies, which saw dice rolled onto a mat with symbols, offering the chance to win - or lose money. Brian took a keen look at this and other games, as he had a gut feeling that this pursuit might possibly provide him with a proper income as his own boss. He also realised that going to sea was great way of life, but he would always be working for someone, as well as answering to whatever demands they decided, or even being sacked for whatever spurious reason. The next part of his travels saw him return to a favourite city, along with some unusual purchases from the Far East, many of which raised a laugh with his ship buddies, but this perceptive Kiwi would soon have the last laugh....

Chapter 5 THE GAMBLER

Many seafarers like to spend their wages ashore, in many ways, such as the pursuit of hitting the fleshpots of the racy ports or buying quality clothes at very low prices. Some buy tacky tourist trinkets or souvenirs that will remind them of wherever they landed, whilst others have more perceptive ways of using their hard-earned wedges. Many eyebrows were raised, along with a few laughs as Brian struggled up the odd gangplank, carrying an assortment of unusual furniture that was to be stored in the large cargo areas, to be offloaded at a later port of call. Tables, chairs and the like were very cheap out in the Far East, as well as being of a much higher quality than British made goods, but these purchases were all part of a plan that filled Brian's head. As soon as the ship docked at Southampton, Brian offloaded his latest collection at the quayside, then arranging the transport for his latest additions to be whisked off into a local storage facility.

His shipmates ribbed him, but Brian took it all in good faith as he laughed it all off, collecting more bits on each journey. They all thought that perhaps this sailor merely wished to set up as a furniture salesman, leaving the sea life behind him as he settled down to a life of a landlubber. Nothing could be further from the truth, as the wily young man made more enquiries on each regular visit back to Southampton. He knew that there was money to be made, by selling the stylish furniture to make a decent profit, but he had other ideas bubbling around his head. His main vision was to open a small club, using this very furniture as a temporary setup, before progressing to bigger things as and when this first gamble took off. The dreams were just around the corner, as the next few amazing years would prove. In between the Nevasa sailings, Brian also joined the R.M.S. Caronia, also known as 'The Green Goddess' which formed part of the prestigious Cunard fleet of liners.

This wonderful liner was used for cruising, as well as on the busy Transatlantic crossings from Southampton to New York, along with the classic Queen Mary and Queen Elizabeth, that have both passed into maritime history. In fact, he had a spell on the Mary, way down in the galleys as he washed pots, pans, cutlery and plates that had seen the finest meals served to several millionaires up above. Brian worked hard in the kitchens as a dishwasher, a few decks below the prosperous passengers who enjoyed first class dining and all that goes with the luxury of the classic liners. It raises a smile, as within a few short years, Brian found himself seated above, being waited on hand and foot, but never forgetting where he came from, as he toiled in a hot sweaty kitchen down in the depths. Sharing cramped crew cabins was also part of life on the ocean waves, but all part of the memories that stayed with him later in life. He was also more than generous when tipping any crew on his later travels, respecting the hard work undertaken by those who chose the vocation, never forgetting where he came from. Brian also recalls celebrating his 21st birthday in 1955 with a bottle of beer, being very hard up at the time. He made up with a few more drinks throughout his Merchant Navy days, with its hard drinking culture, although he has always been a moderate drinker throughout his life.

Another memory was around the age of 22, when Brian was working for the Union Castle line, in the galley of the M.V. Stirling Castle, on the Cape Run to South Africa. He got into a fight with a big thick-set Irish guy on board, giving him a good hiding, as befits a former national boxing champion! The poor guy didn't know what hit him. When the ship docked back in Southampton, the sore loser went ashore, before returning with three of his burly Irish mates in tow, inviting Brian to step off the ship onto the quayside, by shouting at the galley area where he was still on duty. The porthole opened, and Brian popped his head out, shouting back, saying he would be there *"in a couple of minutes"* to face up to the challenge. Picking up two large carving knives from the pantry, he strolled casually down the gangplank, into the shadow of a large crane where the four Paddies lay waiting for some retribution. Holding up the weapons, he said *"I have one – who wants the other one?"* They beat a hasty retreat, and Brian was never bothered by the same guy again, who avoided him at all costs.

Landing back in Southampton after another trip, Brian decided that washing thousands of dishes in the bowels of a ship was not really the ideal way to earn a crust. He cast his eye on another avenue of opportunity, by applying for a training course as a marine radio operator - a far more prestigious means of employment. It could also result in an officer status, with a smart uniform to go with the job, with the bonus of attracting the ladies. A few miles out of Southampton lies the suburb of Hamble, close to the river of the same name that flows out to the Solent and beyond. The School of Marine Radio and Radar (AST) saw the twenty one year old back 'at school' knuckling down to the complex world of global communication, learning about radio frequencies, Morse Code and much more. Quite a daunting task, especially for one whose early academic achievements were not as successful as he had wished for.

The goal was to attain the rank of ship's radio officer, including seagoing courses in Marconi Radio and Radar, along with other facets that needed technical expertise of a high calibre. Many trainees dropped out at the early stages, which is not surprising as any position at sea saw any radio operator in charge of communications, upon which the safety of the whole vessel would depend on. No surprise when Brian joined the ranks of the outside world again, looking for pastures new back in the town centre. He was also enjoying the carnal pleasures of the local girls who fell for his good looks, accent and natural charm, aided by smooth-talking chat-up lines that often ended up in a bed somewhere. For a short while, he also worked part-time at the open air Southampton Lido swimming pool as a lifeguard, thus providing more chances to mingle with scantily-clad girls sunning themselves, or taking a dip. Money was another main reason for not completing the course, thus curtailing this latest episode in his life.

Undeterred by his recent experiences in Hamble, Brian needed to find any kind of employment, so took up a vacancy as a labourer in a warehouse–not a whorehouse! He got on well with his new boss, working hard albeit for a low wage, but within a short time he felt the time was right to hint at a small increment in the pay-packet. When the two were alone in the office, Brian raised the issue but was not very happy with the negative response, as the company finances did not warrant any raise in wages for anyone. The manager knew that he had a good worker in front of him, unlike the rest of the team that did not pull their weight as much as this young Kiwi, but who was now threatening to leave straight away. After a few more minutes, the boss smiled and acknowledged that this fresh-faced lad was an asset to the firm, thus granting him a small increase in his weekly wage. However, on the way out Brian was told that this was 'very confidential', so not to be disclosed to anyone else around the factory, for fear of a backlash with more demands for parity. The other workers noticed Brian's demeanour, bordering on cockiness that soon attracted the attention whilst they all sat at the canteen table on the lunch break. The cat was soon out of the proverbial bag as Brian let it slip that he had wangled a rise, which naturally incensed his latest workmates.

The inevitable demands for the same rise reached the boss, who was furious with Brian for betraying the confidence of the secret arrangement. Tempers were raised, with the threat of downing tools and an imminent walkout by the whole workforce, so it was just a matter of time before Brian got his marching orders, being the only way out for the employers. Once again, being unemployed raised his awareness that any kind of work carried the risk of being kicked out of any job, on the whim of any superior in the pecking order of any firm or ship. It was time for a big step in life, which offering the chance of him being his own boss, in charge of his own destiny at last. It would be another gamble, but this word underlines what has been a common denominator throughout the last few decades.

Chapter 6 SOUTHAMPTON

The time and the place were just right for Brian's next step as he settled in Southampton - one of the most famous ports in the world. Post-war austerity was giving way to a new 'golden age' in which the world was determined to rebuild itself. The mid-Fifties with the new wave of rock n roll music and movies from America, ignited the flames of rebellion with the younger British generation. The word 'teenager' kicked in as they turned their backs on their parents' way of life, as well as having money in their jeans pockets with ever increasing prosperity improving our way of life.

The two main Southampton Docks were full of ships from across the world, with cargo vessels bringing the new goods that had been denied for so many years due to the ravages of war, as well as the luxury liners, carrying their well-heeled passengers. Many Hollywood and other visiting movie stars passed through the city, as well as visiting pop stars such as Bill Haley and The Comets who triggered riots as they left RMS Queen Elizabeth onto the waiting London-bound train at the nearby Terminus station in 1957. The sister ship, RMS Queen Mary, was the another legendary liner that graced our shores, before she was retired to start a new life at Long Beach California back in 1967, whilst 'The Lizzie' met a sad ending in Hong Kong harbour in 1972.

The city's convenient location and double tide has provided a great harbour over the centuries, from around 70 AD when the Romans settled alongside the River Itchen at a place that they named Clausentum. The next few centuries witnessed the growth of the Anglo-Saxon region of Wessex, with Winchester taking over as the second capital of England, as Roman Colchester faded away. Modern Southampton's long history really took off following the Norman invasion of the 11th century. This resulted in massive building of fortifications, laying out the foundations for the ensuing centuries, as other foreign counties tried to invade our shores, notably the French from across the Channel. King Henry V passed by the old town, on his way to fight our near neighbours at Agincourt in 1415, as well as many brave armies some 500 years later, as we faced the threat of invasion from another country in 1914 and 1939.

Southampton was fast becoming a busy shipping thoroughfare, firmly establishing itself over the last couple of centuries as the docks grew out of the ancient harbour into the old and new locations. Passenger liners saw a decline during the Sixties as the new age of air travel provided holidaymakers with a chance of foreign holidays, as well as offering the benefit of crossing the Atlantic in a few hours, as opposed to a few days by sea. This also naturally appealed to the business community as the world was shrinking fast.

During the Fifties, many British families decided to make the decision of a new life on the other side of the world, as Australia and New Zealand offered new opportunities. Just ten old pounds was the heavily subsidised fare out to a new world of sunshine with guaranteed employment that certainly appealed to many young families that had suffered years of deprivation during, and after the second war. These 'Ten Pound Poms' sailed away down Southampton Water in their thousands, with hopes, dreams and aspiration of a better life, but yet another gamble in life. Two other well-known ships are connected with Southampton as the Mayflower docked for a short while in 1620, as she sailed onto Plymouth and the New World.

These early settlers, known as the Pilgrim Fathers, paved the way for the fledgling country that eventually became the major power within some 400 years, but cementing the USA and UK with a special relationship. Another well-known liner set sail in the same direction back in 1912, carrying a mix of billionaires and impoverished immigrant settlers, which sadly ended the lives of some 1500 souls in the freezing waters of the North Atlantic. The late twentieth century saw a rise in the cruise industry, firmly establishing Southampton as a major world terminal with more and more large ships sailing into this fine port. Its container port is also a major part of the local economy, although this led to the decline of manual dock labour when this new advance in freight gradually changed the profile.

The old part of the city is only a few minutes' walk away from either of the two main docks, with many marvellous old buildings dating back to the Middle Ages. Sadly, its location resulted in heavy bombing by the German Luftwaffe during the war years as they targeted the docks, railways and nearby Spitfire factory. As well as the terrible casualties and damage across the city, there was also the added risk of North Atlantic convoys that were at the mercy of the German U-Boats, as they made their perilous way across the ocean. Many brave merchant seamen lost their lives as part of the war effort, helping to bring much needed cargo to our embattled shores. The proximity of the main centre to the port area has always provided the opportunity for visiting crew members to let off steam, in between the sailing schedules. This has happened all over the world, as randy sailors flock to the local pubs, bars and clubs in search of wine, women and song! Some of them had been on board for weeks at a time, so headed off with wedges of cash to spend having fun, in between a few brawls or run-ins with the police. However, Southampton was never a 'wild' kind of place and I recall how busy the various watering holes were. My teenage years allowed me the opportunity to have some great nights, when visiting the pubs and bars all over town, but never on a par with the visiting crew members from all over the world!

If you take a walk up from the old Royal Pier gatehouse, it takes you up through Bugle Street into St Michael's Square which is overlooked by its own wonderful named building on the right. St Michael's Church is the oldest building in Southampton that is still in use, dating back to the late 11th century on the site of the original church. On the other side of the square lies Tudor House, another famous landmark that has housed a museum for many years, and this area was lucky enough not to have been bombed in the last war. It is said that the German pilots used the church spire as a navigational guide on their deadly missions during the Blitz, and that they had orders not to drop their bombs on that part of the city. As you look across the square, you will note a small alley on the right of the church that leads into Castle Way that runs down from the nearby city centre. On that spot stood one of the finest nightclub casinos that Southampton has ever boasted, and there has never been another such venue to rival the heydays of the Swinging Sixties, through the Seventies and a few years on before coming to a sad end.

St Michaels' Square 2018

This aerial photograph looks down on St Michael's church, showing the remaining 'Tudor' frontage of the old Silhouette Club in the middle of the image. Castle Way is on the left, which has an alleyway leading to the old site of the club, passing by the side of the church. The large Tudor House museum can be seen on the right of the square, with Bugle Street leading down to the waterfront, and the Red Funnel Ferries Terminal for the Isle of Wight services. Thanks to the local Kuti family, the old 1930s Royal Pier gatehouse has been preserved, housing their very popular Asian restaurant, but with the derelict eyesore of the old pier jetty in the background. The top of the image shows the Town Quay, so all of these sights were seen by our former sailor as he visited Southampton in those far off days. The city centre is only a few hundred yards away, so this was the perfect location for a tiny club that soon emerged as one of the South's top nightspots, as the newest arrival set about his dreams.

Site of The Silhouette Club- November 2017

    The town was granted a Royal Charter in 1964, which gave its new city status but many of us locals still talk about "going to town" with the Silhouette Club becoming a popular feature during this time. Sadly, I never visited this club during my early years on various pub crawls, but everybody knew about the place and some of my local musician pals along with DJs performed there, with their own great memories. Southampton was very lucky to see this former merchant seaman fall in love with her, as it was all part of Kiwi's outstanding contribution to the area, apart from making his own fortune. The next few years saw a very basic pipedream grow into the busiest club in the area, with its new entrepreneur going from strength to strength.

Chapter 7 KING OF CLUBS

The King of Clubs is the perfect playing card that is often highlighted by those who look deeper into symbolism, with this following description that seems to cover our budding businessman. Taken from one of many websites, which more or less fits the subject of this book:

Wonderfully creative and a very fast learner, even the careless and negative King of Clubs has keen intelligence and insight. The King of Clubs is also known as an emotional idealist and needs to be careful they don't scatter their forces due to emotional disturbances and problems within the family. The King of Clubs rarely lacks money and they usually make it by being in business for themselves.

After his various disappointments, at the mercy of previous employers, Brian was by now ready to take a massive leap forward, striking out on his own and ready to make a mark on the world. Ever the perceptive type, he looked around his adopted home town, realising that there was a gap in the leisure market. 1960 was a pivotal year, as the Swinging Sixties were slowly gaining ground, with fuller employment that improved the lives of many people, as well as boosting the disposable income on consumer goods, better housing and much more. Southampton was full of pubs, but sadly lacking in any kind of nightclub scene that usually caters for the more prosperous types. Many bars frowned on unaccompanied female customers and many more were hardly the kind of place to take a lady out for the night, especially in the rougher areas.

There was a gap in the market, that this latest immigrant realised, and having visited a few overseas ports he envisaged a nightclub where the better-off kind of customer could relax in safe surroundings. He naturally knew that visiting seamen had money to burn, budgeting for booze plus a flutter at cards or on any gaming tables, as well as catching the eye of any young ladies that might lead to unleashing a few weeks of sexual frustration at sea. His dreams of a good location centred around the harbours of the Old and New Docks, thus creating a diversion for the visiting mariners and passengers on their way to and from the ships. Although being very close to the main town area, he scouted around for suitable premises at affordable rents and rates.

By 1960, this twenty six year old Kiwi had saved up around £300 (nearly £5,000 in current money) as well as having a decent collection of his own privately imported furniture stored near the docks. The quality of this foreign collection could have been sold at a decent profit, as it was unusual for those times, so would have attracted wealthy buyers who wanted something out of the ordinary. Tucked away in the corner of St Michaels Square, next to the church was the perfect location for this new enterprise as Brian forged ahead with his dream. The former warehouse was leased for £6 a week (£100 current money) as Brian took yet another gamble with his life savings to sink into this venture, which was scary but exciting for him.

His next step was to find a friendly bank manager, with the aim of securing an overdraft that might help establish a firm ground to launch his dream idea. The first three banks were not impressed by his pitch, youth and lack of collateral, but this did not deter this confident lad who was barely out of his teens, shrugging off these early attempts as mere setbacks.

Next on the list was the small local District Bank, which was later taken over by the National Westminster group, as were many of the lesser banks around the country. Brian was ushered into Eric Wood's office, sitting down at the large desk, then proceeded to lay out his plans, plus projected figures, with the confidence of a much older businessman. Eric was immediately impressed with Brian on a personal level, although the bank executives were not known for being too generous with new clients, so he felt rather cautious at first. However, Brian won him over with his enthusiasm and his ability to communicate, which is an important part of any potential club owner profile. Handshakes sealed a deal that set him on course into the later multi-millionaire status. Some while after this meeting, as the new business was getting off the ground, Eric and Brian met up for a drink and friendly chat. Brian casually asked why he was granted this all important overdraft and extra banking facilities. Eric smiled, explaining that Brian had mentioned his early years as a teenage champion boxer. This impressed him, as he knew full well that he was dealing with a real fighter and a genuine person not let him or the bank down.

His reasonable savings and general manner had impressed this perceptive bank manager, who had no hesitation in granting him the facilities that established him as a respectable new businessman. Securing the help of a handyman and other helpers, Brian set about with this ambitious venture that very soon attracted the kind of clientele that boosted the profile, providing a classy nightclub. His time at sea had given him ideas of what people liked, from the luxury liners to the various ports that he had visited. The layout of ship's casinos and restaurants also inspired him to invest in upmarket décor, creating the right atmosphere with suitable lighting and all that goes with it. It needed a name, so after some thought of all the places he had been or read about, Brian decided on a title – The Flamingo Club. Partly inspired by the world famous complex in Las Vegas, that would also see him frequent the city's casinos after making his own fortunes with his own gaming tables, this was perfect. It is well known that the 'Mob' founded the most famous 'Sin City' in the late Forties on, as large areas of former desert evolved into what we see these days. 'Bugsy' Siegel along with many more big shady characters invested their ill-gotten gains into casinos and clubs along the famous Strip, before the authorities clamped down to clean the city up.

There was also a very successful English club of that name, founded in Soho back in 1952, as a music-based club featuring jazz, followed by the r&b boom of the early Sixties. Brian liked the idea of importing a taste of London, located some seventy odd miles up the old A33, honing in on the new wave of entertainment that would keep the tills busy. He was not one to cut corners as such, but kept a keen eye on costs which saw a certain degree of second hand items being utilised in the early days, but firmly intending to upgrade what was necessary as and when the club took off. These shrewd moves certainly worked, and the club soon took shape as everybody worked round the proverbial clock to meet the deadline. Carefully positioned drapes covered otherwise plain walls, with a panelled ceiling plus wall to wall carpeting setting the scene.

Brian's own furniture came out of storage, mixed with other purchased equipment, as well as trendy lighting that added to the overall image that he had planned for a long time. Padded studded leather bars also exuded a taste of luxury, with a wide display of spirits and exotic cocktails. Brian had negotiated a 'sale or return' with his liquor merchants, along with other clever arrangements that certainly paid off in the long run. He was also gaining a much-needed commodity - respect. This soon paid off as the next move was to apply for a much-coveted gaming licence which was eventually granted, thus enabling him to upgrade to casino operation. This took a couple of years as the Flamingo Club settled down with a growing reputation, plus an ever expanding membership.

No expense was spared, especially on the ladies' powder rooms, as they were called, certainly impressing those who 'spent a penny' but spent many pounds back in the main rooms! His sea-faring days had given him some good ideas to little details that impressed the passengers, so now they were put to good use in his new venture.

Near to the opening date, Brian had acquired a small staff, many of whom stayed with their new boss for many years to come, as well as becoming good friends. His maritime catering background fared well as he oversaw the food supplies, as well as making sure of recruiting a top chef plus a smartly dressed crew that offered that all important first impression when any customer walked into this building.

Kiwi had landed on his feet, at the right time and place, with his ambitions all coming to fruition–not that easy in those days as lending/borrowing was difficult with very few people having any collateral to back them up when trying to get bank loans or credit. Very few owned their homes or even had a car, so he had achieved a lot in a short time. He cast his mind back to Upper Hutt, where very few people had made anything out of life, progressing from school into the drudgery of ordinary employment that merely kept them ticking over until retirement. The opening night was a great success, thanks to local advertising plus word of mouth amongst Brian's new business contacts, as they were all excited about the whole concept.

Within a short time, the business was booming as the Flamingo became the place to be seen, as part of being in with the 'In Crowd' to coin a Sixties expression. This endearing club owner was not the type that stayed in the shadows, being the perfect host and front man who made the effort to meet, greet and smooth talk his new customers into enjoying great nights out. Kiwi soon became the talk of the town, as news of this glitzy venue spread far and wide.

Live entertainment goes hand in hand with casino/nightclubs, which saw Brian booking the right kind of acts to suit his club members. They enjoyed fine food, followed by star cabaret that featured local and 'big name' acts, including Danny Williams, whose 'Moon River' hit had topped the UK charts in 1961. A rare signed photo shows him onstage – the 'casual' style with cigarette and whisky in hand, accompanied by the resident jazz pianist and trumpet player, being part of the band who also entertained the room. The atmosphere was building nicely, with increased numbers through the door as the Flamingo's reputation was growing day by day.

Kiwi's plans were working well, as the profits were being paid back into the business in readiness for the next stage, allowing him the chance to improve and expand the popular venue. An old wine shop stood next to the Flamingo, which had caught Brian's attention as he noticed that their trading seemed rather quiet. He still thinks back to those early times, feeling that he may have had a premonition, when passing by these premises on a daily basis.

On a hunch, he called by to casually enquire if the owners were thinking of selling up – which they were! This then allowed for the expansion needed, in order for the new casino room to be added onto the existing lower main club area. Another mix of luck at the right time and the right place – more or less a template for his charmed life!

Danny Williams

As anticipated, the visiting sailors came in droves, often recommended on the Merchant Navy grapevine, as each crew wanted to know where to go on their shore visits. The more prosperous local townspeople became regular visitors, with Brian remembering their first names and all snippets of information. This personal touch reaped its rewards, boosting his reputation along with the Flamingo that saw off its new rival establishments that cropped up, but often failed.

The Flamingo Casino area near opening night

The new gaming area lacked the sparkle of the rest of the Flamingo, offering a very basic set-up of chairs and playing tables, so Brian knew that this had to be upgraded as soon as possible to enhance the whole experience. He also envisaged expanding the premises, after many a successful evening that saw the club gaining popularity. It was all part of his plan, as it was all working well enough to move onwards and upwards.

The young female bar staff were also very attractive–all part of the equation for any successful nightclub, as well as the pretty croupiers who attracted many a wandering male eye, thus making them stay longer at the gaming tables.

Home-made roulette table!

The Blackjack table was knocked up by the handyman, with the playing surface cut out to accommodate the players' area. As for the Roulette table – this was also home-made with the plastic wheel purchased from the nearby W.H. Smith shop! By now, his bank manager was more than satisfied with his new customer, a brash young confident businessman who was quite a contrast to the usual type of older conservative types. A meeting was arranged, in order to request a much-needed loan as the current turnover was steady, but not looking too good in the long term. The banker shared Kiwi's optimism as well as casting a keen eye on his figures and good book-keeping via a respected accountant over the early years. The newly acquired building also allowed for the new downstairs Kiwi Restaurant to open, with the new gaming area in readiness above the premises, Once again, success breeds success as the daytime trade also drifted into early evening, linking in nicely with the nightclub side of it all.

He ran a tight ship, but was firm and fair when dealing with staff as a degree of discipline is required in any business. If people didn't pull their weight in whatever job they were doing, or causing any rift in the workplace, then they were soon out of the door. He also made a few 'enemies' as does any successful person, but usually restricted to sore losers at the gaming tables, or by disgruntled ex-staff whose standards were not up to the Kiwi levels. The Flamingo had run its early course, with a bigger bolder expansion waiting in the wings, as the upstairs area was now ready to be utilised, providing Southampton with its most iconic club and a name that has gone down in local modern history.

A new year and a new club name was the next step, which set the ball rolling as Brian upped his game plan to boost his venue to even bigger things, as well as his growing bank balance.

Chapter 8 THE SILHOUETTE CLUB

1963 was an amazing year as a new word was coined that heralded a renaissance in popular music and culture in general. Beatlemania, with its offshoots woke the world up as the earlier charts were dominated by 'safe' American singers and groups, with wholesome images. The Merseybeat sound followed on, and within a year, the music had been repackaged, then shipped back across the Atlantic as part of the British Invasion. English heavyweight champion boxer Henry Cooper floored Cassius Clay, whom Brian met some years later, after Clay changed his name to Mohammed Ali. 1963 is also remembered for the Profumo scandal, as the sexual antics of Christine Keeler helped to bring down the government of the day. The Great Train Robbery, along with the Kennedy assassination in November of that year, was another main story, so everything was changing fast.

St Michaels Square also changed that year, as the brand new Silhouette Club replaced the old Flamingo Club. The bank's wise choices to back this new kid on the block had paid off, as Brian ploughed more of the profits into a complete renovation of the upper and lower floors. The loans were paid back within a short time, as the club went from strength to strength with an ever increasing national recognition. It was out with the old gaming tables, and in with the new equipment, including expensive roulette tables imported from Paris, along with classy furniture that enhanced the whole experience for the ever growing membership list.

The much-coveted gaming licence application was granted, followed by mass advertising and a massive boost to the new club's membership. The Flamingo had run its course, gaining a great reputation around the area in the early days, but now Kiwi was stepping up his game with this new venture.

Silhouette Club – The Sixties

The new look – nothing home-made now!

The Swinging Sixties saw the refurbished Silhouette Club become a magnet for a wide mix of a clientele, from 'ordinary' Sotonians, plus many local professional football players as The Saints team were also getting bigger wage packets. Local business people were regular customers, rubbing shoulders with many celebrities who were passing by. Big name chart-topping stars that were appearing at local theatres and dance halls were given VIP status, as well as visiting television and movie stars. These celebrities appreciated being able to unwind in relaxing surroundings, without being pestered by other club-goers, unlike modern times when every little thing they do is recorded on phones, or by the ever present paparazzi. The invasion of privacy is a modern phenomenon, so one can only imagine the relief of the big names of that era as they let their hair down when needed, away from prying eyes.

The larger gaming area with the cashier kiosk on the left side of the photograph above. Always the perfectionist, Brian went to great lengths to ensure that every detail was just right, improving all the time as he had done his 'homework' in previous years. He had made notes of the various clubs and casinos on his many travels, translating them into every new plan of the Silhouette layout.

A personal invitation from Brian Adamson—founder and Managing Director:

It has been my aim to establish, here in the South, a Businessmen's Rendezvous worthy of the size and growth of industry and commerce within the area. In combining the facilities of both Casino and Silhouette Clubs, I have established a new and long-needed level of sophistication in business entertainment. I hope you will visit the Club and meet us personally.

Lower gaming area

Silhouette brochure

December 1964 saw a major publicity coup for the Silhouette Club, as a brand new pop group from Birmingham were at the Southern TV studios at Northam, on the banks of the River Itchen that runs down to the Solent. The Moody Blues were celebrating the release of their first single 'Go Now' which was a great cover of an American r&b hit, that saw them hit the number one spot in the UK charts, as well as reaching high spots around the world. They asked where was the best place in the area, where they could party the night away, so it was naturally off to St Michaels Square and an amazing evening carried on till the early hours.

THE MOODY BLUES *Decca Records*

Brian's autographed flyer

    The Moody Blues were fronted by Denny Laine on bass and vocals, but he was later replaced by lead vocalist Justin Hayward, whose song-writing talents led the group to even bigger global status. "Nights in White Satin" was a world-wide smash hit in 1967, along with many more singles and progressive albums that dominated the later years. 1967 was known as 'the summer of love' and Brian had been having these for a long time before – many in white satin! Denny Laine was later part of Paul McCartney's new band, as Wings carried on the great tradition from the Fab Four era. The Merseybeat explosion also saw

Gerry Marsden appear at the Silhouette – the first group to have their first three singles hit the no.1 spot in the UK charts. Quite fitting to perform at the no. 1 club of course.

Gerry and the Pacemakers

Local pop groups were also booked to play at the Silhouette, along with DJs, creating a great atmosphere that very few other rival clubs could match. The superior food side gained a wide reputation, as Brian's former experiences on the catering element came into play, along with the bar set-up, so he knew that the whole package was working well. He also made sure that the door security men were well trained in diplomacy and tact, especially when dealing with any problems with 'difficult' customers. They were not bouncers in the traditional manner, unlike many establishments who employed the 'gorilla' types to intimidate any awkward inebriated idiots that were trying to gain entry. On the odd occasion, Brian was called out to the entrance to check on any such problems, in order to placate the nuisance who would not take no for an answer. The idiot often demanded to *"see the manager!"*, followed by a few words, a flare-up with the poor sap being knocked halfway across St Michaels Square by a well-aimed right hook, courtesy of a former national boxing champion! Many club members will recall the polite but firm doormen, including 'Big Richard' whose size had an immediate effect in quelling any hint of trouble.

Kiwi ran a tight ship, with very little trouble that might blemish the club's reputation, thus creating a rapport with the local police, who were more than satisfied with this particular nightclub. The Silhouette was more like a family firm, as Brian made sure that the working conditions and wages matched the hard work as well as everybody getting on well with each other. The club atmosphere was just right, appealing to a wide spectrum of local members and their guests – many of them took out a membership as well after just one visit. Food and service were uppermost, with every little detail taken care of as Kiwi did his rounds on every night when he was back in town.

The Silhouette also felt safe for the club-goers, with very little trouble flaring up apart from the odd drunk or a losing gambler – often the same combination. Brian also knew which kind of entertainment suited his clientele, so often re-booking local groups, singers, DJs and all manner of artistes that many of the club members enjoyed. Not forgetting the many big stars that appeared at the Silhouette or merely passed by, when they were performing in the area. The feedback from these successful nights were talked about the next day in many a workplace, thus providing more PR that resulted in even busier nights. This provided even more advertising on top of the normal press articles in the local press, so it all ran like clockwork.

Chapter 9 THE GOLDEN YEARS

The Silhouette was enjoying the boom years of the Sixties, thanks to the profits from the casino side which helped to pay for the diverse entertainment that made for the perfect evening, along with food and drink income. In amongst the pop music provided by the beat groups, plus the disc jockeys that played the right kind of music to please all ages and genres, there was also a thriving jazz night that catered for that eclectic taste. These were billed as 'Modern Jazz' nights, attracting a more sedate kind of audience, who just wanted to sit, watch and listen to smooth music. The same types also tended to drink more, unlike the 'Trad Jazz' crowd with more people staying on the dance floor. This was the more lively side of the genre which was very popular in the early Sixties. Brian alternated these two jazz nights, thus pleasing both camps, not forgetting that the dancers developed a thirst whilst jiving away to the band. It also made for a good atmosphere plus he was able to book some well-known names such as Kenny Ball and his Jazzmen – one of the top UK acts at the time.

Always looking at other options, Brian saw a gap during the quieter mid-week, so decided to raise his game by introducing cabaret style entertainment on an otherwise 'dead' Tuesday night, resulting in even more incredible nights at the South's top venue. The club was also booked for private parties, business launches, meetings along with other lucrative functions. The new Tuesday Cabaret Nights soon took off, featuring top class artistes who loved performing in the intimate surroundings, with atmosphere to match. Comedians, singers and all kinds of acts graced the stage, as well as the usual visiting entertainers who were appearing elsewhere in the town, or should we say city by now. Brian was himself a proud new citizen in his own new setting.

Although Kiwi had established a good relationship with the authorities, plus an excellent reputation as a responsible club-owner, he was often frustrated by the council's stubbornness when applying for permission for 'special' occasions. Added problems came about, due to nearby residents who wrongly blamed the Silhouette members for 'disrupting' the late nights when leaving the premises. This would all later result in a major decision to sell up in the late Eighties.

Ann Palmer with the Sean the chef and Brian- special buffet!

Kiwi checking the bar takings- the smile says it all

The likes of top acts such as The Tremeloes, Edison Lighthouse, Danny Williams, Swinging Blue Jeans and many more top artistes boosted the profile. There were very few other clubs in the area that featured the bigger names in show-business, so Brian had hit on the right formula.

£1 Silhouette casino chip

Brian still laughs at the memory of the time when one of the UK's top comedians walked through the door, as he was appearing at a local theatre. Waving his tickling stick around, with hair sticking up and cracking gags through his well-known teeth, Ken Dodd had the club-goers in stitches for most of the evening. Kiwi recalls Doddy waltzing in through the front entrance, with his nose twitching and sniffing the air, with one of his great lines *"By Jove Missus - this place has atmosphere!"*

One notable regular visitor was a major star attraction, lauded as Britain's answer to Marilyn Monroe in the voluptuous blonde bombshell shape of Diana Dors. A former Swindon girl, who had sensibly changed her real name, to become a big name in the Fifties onward as an actress, singer and cabaret performer. One of her many humorous quotes being:

"They asked me to change my name. I suppose they were afraid that if my real name Diana Fluck was in lights and one of the lights blew......"

Diana had been signed up by the Rank Organisation, appearing in low budget comedy/sexy roles in various movies, gaining quite a raunchy reputation over the next few years. Her personal life was sadly tarnished by a series of misfortunes, including her first husband's handling of her financial affairs. She married Dennis Hamilton in 1951, who then used all manner of publicity stunts to push her name into the tabloid press, plus nude photo-shoots that cemented her status as a sex symbol. Her next screen outing was 'Lady Godiva Rides Again' being the perfect soft porn movie, amusing many who knew how the title fitted the star! There was talk of Hamilton 'lending' his gorgeous wife out to leading film producers of the day, in return for favours that could be labelled as the casting couch route to bigger things, much in the news these days. Diana had a series of misfortunes, firstly being ripped off by her unscrupulous husband, followed by more heavy financial losses by one of her lovers. Her short-lived success in the USA, with movies and cabaret appearances saw her move back to England, to carry on with various television and movie roles through the Sixties.

She also appeared on the nightclub circuit, which eventually led her to the Silhouette Club, immediately bonding with Kiwi, as they laughed and shared X-rated stories well into the early hours after each barnstorming show of music and comedy. Brian loved blondes as *"they got dirtier quicker!"* Diana, like Brian, was a survivor and a fighter, thus cementing a friendship that lasted many years as the two of them had common ground. Brian was also to become a 'victim' of unsavoury financial dealings within a few years, as this story will later reveal.

A pair of sex symbols!

Diana mixed with an amazing variety of celebrities, from movie stars to royalty, as well as being a regular visitor to the Kray-owned nightclubs in London, plus other 'shady' locations that later formed part of her autobiographies. Despite her previous downfalls, she soon re-established herself, selling many stories to the tabloid press as well as being a regular participant on television chat shows, where her great chat and natural humour endeared her to newer audiences. Diana was also well-known for hosting raucous 'adult' parties at her luxurious house in Sunningdale Berkshire, with many well-known faces in discreet attendance. A well-know comedian was one of her regular visitors, joking about these hedonistic drink and drug-filled parties with one of his gags *"The only trouble with an orgy – you don't know who to thank on the way out....."*

Kiwi's well-honed profile as a self-publicist was also well to the fore, keeping the local press informed of which well-known names might be gracing his establishment, with open invitations to journalists, to visit the club, sampling the hospitality that paid dividends and extra marketing/PR coverage. This had come about, when he recalled his formative years as a teenage boxing champion, who had gained local media interest in a small town, as well as his close shave with the Grim Reaper on that fateful day when his train crash sparked early reporting. Clouds were gathering on the horizon, in the shape of the British Gaming Board, which was taking a long hard look at the legislation across all areas, as betting shops had become legalised from the early Sixties. Horse racing also witnessed a massive upturn as more punters upped their stakes, providing the bookies with higher revenues, all part of the equation that boosted the government tax coffers. Casinos also sprung up over those early years, but many were found to be covers for criminal activity, as money-laundering became a new buzz word, enabling hard cash to be moved around quite easily in the black economy.

There were also concerns that the American Mafia was taking a keen interest in the UK casino trade, on the lines that had seen the emergence of Las Vegas, founded in part by the mobsters, including 'Bugsy' Siegel back in the 1940s, with his own Flamingo Club! Unlike many casinos, Brian kept the maximum bets to a reasonable £10, later upped to £20, which deterred some of the 'high roller' types but still enjoying healthy profits throughout the years. In addition, he kept a close watch on those punters who were losing far too much at the tables. This often causes problems for certain types who can ill afford major losses. Kiwi never 'chased bets' when at the tables, knowing when to walk away.

The later years saw even more legislation being introduced, with growing concerns over some club managers, many of whom were often front men for shady characters. The Silhouette was definitely not in this category, keeping meticulous records that fell under the scrutiny of top accountants, as well as keeping the local tax office happy with the submitted books at the end of every financial year. The club's gaming tables and fruit machines (one-armed bandits) kept a steady cash flow during these boom years, with Kiwi keeping a close eye on what was happening in the industry all over the country. Whilst many rivals were closed down, the Silhouette kept its head above the troubled waters, maintaining its respected position in the community, continuing to thrive through that turbulent decade.

Silhouette Club car windscreen sticker

As one can imagine, the perks of being a young good-looking club owner were adding up all the time, especially when 'pulling the birds' as it was known in those carefree times. Apart from his usual successful chat-up lines, Brian had a number of tricks up his well-tailored sleeves, with a high success rate. Now in his Eighties, he smiles at the nostalgic memory of one of his little escapades to end up bedding yet another beautiful woman. This ruse generally worked more times than not, so the odds were well stacked in the stud's favour. One of his ice-breaking tricks involved a small ladies' purse, containing a ten shilling note. This prop was quickly dropped onto the pavement just as a pretty girl walked past him in the street. Brian's chat-up line followed on with: *"Excuse me Miss, but did you just drop your purse on the ground just now?"*

The response was always negative, but served as an opening gambit. The girl would say no, but it was a conversation opener. Brian then suggested *"Shall we open it to see if there is anything inside that might identify the owner?"* Using the word *"We"* instead of *"I"* was a smooth link to a degree of togetherness, as the purse was opened to reveal the ten bob note, as it was then called. Kiwi then hinted that nobody would claim it, so why not spend the money on a coffee or a drink together? This often led to many hot nights of passion, as well as a few post-coital laughs when the lady cottoned on to the prank, with no hard feelings–apart from the other hard feelings between the sheets! However, one night the target lady thanked Brian, took the purse and strolled off! Win some-lose some.

Kiwi was a workaholic, spending most of his waking hours at the club or overseeing his other investments throughout the day. His property portfolio kept him busy, as he bought up houses, coffee bars, with a small hotel on the horizon. All work and no play was not quite applicable to Brian, as he made sure that regular trips abroad allowed some leisure time. This photo shows him 'twisting' away with a blonde girl at a Majorca night club, leading to more late night fun.

The golden rule for any employer is to avoid relationships with staff, but we are all human, as was a hot-blooded Kiwi on the loose, being surrounded by beautiful women. Brian employed a club manager by the name of Raz, who is still a good friend to this day, with many memories of that time as one can imagine. On one of the usual hectic nights, the staff were trying to cope with packed club, with a queue at the bar and tables waiting to be served. One of the waitresses had gone missing from the main areas for some while, but eventually turned up, looking rather flushed. Raz exploded, demanding to know where the hell she had been, as the staff had been run off their feet yet again. The pretty young thing merely shrugged her shoulders, smiling sweetly, and responded *"What am I supposed to say when YOUR boss has been screwing me on his office desk???"*

These flings were a common occurrence, all part of the Silhouette way of nightlife, enjoyed by both parties with never any degree of coercion on Brian's part. In fact, most of the signals emanated from the steady stream of girls who worked for the club, or being patrons of the Silhouette. All part of the Swinging Sixties, where free love was the name of the game, as many older people still testify with their own fond memories of that era.

Kiwi on the left- keeping an eye

As the club flourished, Brian had no choice but to employ more staff, eventually to around sixty people, the numbers on duty depending on what kind of night saw the demand. One of his earliest staff members, from the 1960 Flamingo days was a hard-working waitress, who later helped out in many other ways around the club, covering extra duties, and often working well past her shifts, but not expecting to get paid overtime. Ann Palmer was then in her late twenties, soon becoming a good friend for many years, as she often took on the responsibility of running the club, whenever Kiwi had to pop out. He knew that she could be relied on, having complete trust in her, which resulted in seeing Ann later being promoted to manageress.

Fast forward to November 2000, after Brian had sold the Silhouette in the late Eighties, as part of his life plan to enjoy the fruits of his success. He was informed that Ann, who was now 68, was in dire need of vital heart surgery, but faced a long waiting list of around eighteen months for a major triple heart by-pass operation. She was married, with two children and living in Brockenhurst, in the New Forest at that time. Without hesitation, Brian offered to pay for private surgery as an early 'Christmas present' leading to a successful outcome a few weeks later as she entered hospital.

This amazing gesture was at the cost of £22,500 (some £36,000 now) but Brian explained it all in a local Hampshire newspaper: *"I opened in 1960. Ann was working for me as a waitress. I used to go out and say 'Ann - look after the place'. As I expanded she became my right arm. If it wasn't for her and the other lovely staff I wouldn't be in the position I am today. I decided to show my appreciation of what she did for me. It's the least I can do for her"*

Boss repays former worker with gift of life
BIG-HEARTED!

By **Sunday Independent reporter**

A KIND-hearted company boss has dipped into his pocket to give a £22,250 gift of life to a former employee.

Brian Adamson made a fortune running Southampton's Silhouette Club with the help of many loyal and trustworthy workers.

And on hearing ex-manageress Ann Palmer needed vital heart surgery he moved to pay for the operation as a gift for Christmas.

Medics told Ann she would have to wait at least 18 months for a triple bypass operation.

But thanks to Brian's generosity she is going into hospital on January 10.

Ann, 66, said: "He is the most fantastic person. There are no words to describe what he is doing for me.

"Brian has given me a new life. Without the operation I may have had five years, now it is ten or 15 years."

Ann, who is married with two children and lives at Brockenhurst in the New Forest, began working for Brian as a waitress at the club when it first opened.

Brian, who now lives abroad, said: "I opened in 1969. Ann was working for me as a waitress. I used to go out and say 'Ann look after the place'. As I expanded she became my right arm."

Over the years Ann rose to become manageress of the club.

He added: "If it wasn't for her and the other lovely staff I wouldn't be in the position I'm in today.

"I decided to show my appreciation of what she did for me. It's the least I can do for her."

DELIGHTED: Ann Palmer with Brian Adamson.

In the article, Ann said *"He is the most fantastic person. There are no words to describe what he is doing for me. Brian has given me a new life. Without the operation I may have five years, now it is ten or fifteen years"* There are many other instances where our philanthropist helped other people, but generally kept it quiet until local news outlets were tipped off.

Chapter 10 BACK TO SEA-WITH A DIFFERENCE!

Brian never forgot his early years, spent in hot steamy ships' galleys, washing pots, pans, plates and cutlery that had often been used on the upper decks in first class restaurants. 1967 was a poignant year for the people of Southampton, as one of the most iconic ocean liners was due to embark on her last journey across the Atlantic Ocean. Along with her younger sister ship, the RMS Queen Elizabeth, the Queen Mary had been a welcome sight on every visit to her home port for some thirty one years since her maiden voyage in 1936, which saw her gain the prestigious Blue Riband Trophy for the fastest crossing a few months later. Apart from transporting the upper echelons of the rich and famous, she had also done her proud bit for the country, as a troop carrier during the war years of 1939 to 1945, but was now operating at a loss, due to air travel taking over, cutting the journey time to just a few hours, instead of days. Whilst many classic liners had met sad endings, in scrap yards or at the bottom of the sea, the 'Mary' was destined for a brand new retirement home in Long Beach California. She has spent the rest of her days as a tourist attraction and museum, attracting millions more visitors over the next decades, as they could experience a taste of British shipping at its best.

As one can imagine, this final trip of a lifetime was way out of reach of most people's pockets, but not for the one-time sailor who saw this as the perfect voyage, and ultimate return to the ocean waves that had first landed him in Southampton. He was accompanied by good pal Allan Grant, another very successful local businessman, rubbing shoulders with just over 1,200 other well-heeled passengers plus some 800 crew, as they sailed out on the 31st October. On this epic voyage, the Mary would not be making her usual trip across the Channel to Cherbourg, with the last leg across to New York, but straight down the Atlantic Ocean. After looping round Cape Horn, on the southern tip of Chile, she then sailed up the South American coast, before docking at Long Beach on the 9th December. Captain John Treasure Jones had the privilege of taking control of this final voyage, having been in charge of the liner for the previous two years. This memorable photograph shows the two VIPs at the front of their fellow first class passengers, as the loyal toast was made in honour of this iconic vessel.

Glasses raised on the Queen Mary final voyage 1967
Brian & Allan at the front beside the captain

The Queen Elizabeth stayed in service for another couple of years, but suffered an awful demise when being sold to a Far East businessman. He had intended to convert her to a floating university, but in 1972 a 'mysterious' fire broke out, as she was moored in Hong Kong Harbour, eventually leading to the mercy of the scrap yard workers. Another 'mysterious' fire was later be part of the Silhouette story, but for now Brian and Allan wallowed in the luxury afforded to them both, as they enjoyed every single day and night aboard this magnificent ship. Having sweated below decks just a few years before, he took every opportunity to explore the stylish Art Deco lounges, bars and restaurants that were out of bounds to most of the crew. Swimming in the two beautiful pools, lounging in the Observation Lounge and sampling top class meals in the First Class Dining Room, known as the Grand Salon filled every day at sea. Brian still has vivid memories of this experience: *"I ate caviar off the same plates that I once washed as a dishwasher, during a stint onboard the same ship as a crew member!"*

Not forgetting where he came from, he made sure that many of his generous tips ended up in the pockets of the hard working galley crew down below, as well as the usual gratuities for the silver service waiters, attending to their every whim. The Verandah Restaurant was turned into the Starlight Room for late night entertainment, so never a dull moment over the weeks as the ship sailed to her final resting place.

The Grand Salon – First Class Dining Room

Brian was also highlighted in an article published in the Sunday People newspaper, by leading columnist Arthur Helliwell, travelling on the ship as part of the press contingent. This was part of his report:

"The most colourful character among 1,270 passengers was Brian Adamson a dapper young man who worked as dishwasher on the ship 10 years ago. Mr Adamson, who now owns the Silhouette Casino in Southampton, was making the round trip wearing ruby and diamond studded domino cufflinks with a flashy £1000 solitaire ring on each

hand. Mr Adamson was of course, exactly the sort of passenger you expected to meet on the Mary in the good old days....."

Brian and Allan – cheers!

Brian and Allan remain good pals to this day, the latter still running one of the top international stamp-dealing businesses from his office in Lyndhurst. Rushstamps (Retail) Ltd was set up back in the Sixties, leading to global success, following on from his younger school days as a keen stamp collector. Just like Brian, young dreams can come true, leading to very successful lifestyles.

All good things come to an end, which saw Kiwi back in Southampton, after this trip of a lifetime, then straight back into making more money with shrewd investments as before. Throughout the Sixties, he had also bought up property in the town, for investment/rental purposes, including a small hotel, as well as a popular coffee bar that sold the most Coca Cola in the South of England at that time! This had been one of his early takeovers, around the same time as the Flamingo Club had morphed into the Silhouette, so this Kiwi was certainly spreading his wings around the area.

The Kasbah was situated on the corner of 74 London Road, below a car sales showroom. A set of stairs, led to the basement, which housed a jukebox, full of the best sounds of the time, making a small fortune for the proprietor. A small cellar had been cleared to make a tiny space, in which local pop groups were able to play in. It was the city's own 'Cavern Club' on a much smaller scale, which brought trade in from all over the area. He was the ultimate workaholic, never standing still for too long, but making time for making love at every opportunity as one of the most eligible bachelors in the city. He also had a flat above the café, enabling him to keep a close watch on the business below, which he retained for several years, used as another office for other businesses.

The trendy Kasbah was a great success, being one of the main meeting places for youngsters in Southampton, until problems kicked in with 'rowdy bikers' leading to neighbour disputes. This was causing too many headaches for this young entrepreneur. After he sold up, the popular venue carried on under new ownership, but then the 'Mods' took over, with more noisy antics in the nearby streets, as their scooters revved up day and night. This eventually led to a 7pm 'curfew' with an early closing time, so Kiwi had got out at the right time – just like his gambling instincts, when knowing when to quit any card game.

1968 was time for the Prodigal Son to make a long mile trip back to his family home in Upper Hutt New Zealand. This was part of a world-wide journey, flying from London to some of his dream destinations that were originally mere drawing pin targets on that old map in his bedroom. It was a 'Busman's Holiday' of sorts as he wanted to take note of international casinos and nightclubs in such places as the Bahamas, Miami, Acapulco, Los Angeles, Las Vegas, Honolulu, Hawaii, Tokyo, Hong Kong, Perth, Sydney. He took everything in, with his usual keen eye, as well as sampling the delights of the gaming tables, plus the obligatory succession of beautiful girls that fell under his spell as a real playboy! Hong Kong was a favourite destination on Brian's travels, reminding him of a trip across the water to Macau, whose economy is based on tourism and gambling. As always, he was making mental notes about the set-up in each of these venues, chatting to the managers when possible. On one occasion, he noted the lack of security on the roulette wheels, as most casinos have inspectors who check the mechanism and required balance. They also keep a close watch on the players, their bets and payouts at the various tables. When Brian queried this with one manager, he was taken aback at the reply "No problem here – if they get caught, they end up swimming with fish in the South China Sea…"

As the decade drew to a close, many casinos were under deep scrutiny by the Gaming Board, thus making it very difficult to open a new venue, or renew the existing licence. Kiwi had steered the Silhouette Club on an even keel for many years, so it was no surprise when the venue was granted one of the very first new licences in Great Britain - no. 9 as can be seen on the certificate. In fact, he was also only one of two private club owners in the UK that had been granted an extension to his existing licence. All down to good management, with no hint of any problems that surround other nightclubs, earning a much-needed commodity - respect.

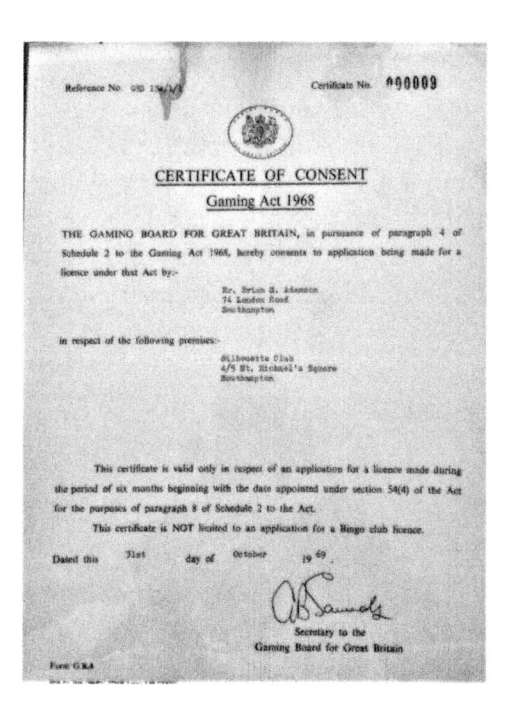

Certificate no. 9

Chapter 11 THE SEVENTIES

New Year's Eve 1969 saw yet another packed house for the best party in town, that carried on till dawn broke over St Michaels Square, as the new decade was ushered in. Brian had his fingers in many proverbial pies, with various investments that paid good dividends all over the city throughout the next ten years. This decade saw much upheaval around the world, with the Middle East oil problems that reverberated all over the globe, resulting in economic chaos. The UK also suffered from militant union strikes, rising prices, inflation and other factors that saw the nation's belt tightened.

Despite the national gloom, people still wanted a good night out, to escape the daily problems, so Kiwi was more than happy to oblige, as the customers kept on coming through the door to spend whatever spare money was available. The wealthier types have always been unaffected, with the classy Silhouetters carrying on as normal as they wined, dined, gambled and danced through the night. Brian never rested on his laurels, keeping the usual eye on the local opposition, as well as plugging the establishment in any way possible. One of his great publicity stunts took place in the late Seventies, as the new Itchen Bridge was opened for the first time, replacing the old Floating Bridges that had been ferrying the locals across the river Itchen for 140 years. This was the link between the suburb of Woolston and the main city centre, so quite a major event for Southampton, leading to much activity in the area.

The work started in 1974, with the new bridge being open for pedestrians on the 31st May 1977, followed by the grand official opening on 13th July by HRH Princess Alexandra, as the civic dignitaries stood around, bristling with pride. One would naturally think that the city mayor and colleagues would lead the procession on this important day, but someone else had different ideas, as an 18th century horse-drawn landau rolled up to steal the show! None other than Brian 'Kiwi' Adamson, resplendent in top hat and tails, breaking out the first of many champagne bottles on this auspicious day. The carriage was festooned with flags plus large signs that showed everybody who was ready to roll across Southampton's latest landmark. This photo shows 'Lord' Adamson having a quick chat with the horseman, as the procession was about to start, with a very pretty lady in tow on the back seat. This beautiful woman was Brian's Thai girlfriend at the time, so turning more heads.

Itchen Bridge Opening 1977

As usual, the local press had been tipped off in advance, which resulted in the Silhouette carriage grabbing the headlines as it managed to squeeze into the front of the procession, leaving a few miffed councillors plus deflated mayor trailing behind! The ensuing publicity boosted the club's profile, as well as being talked about for a very long time after, but one can imagine the atmosphere back in the Civic Centre offices after this little stunt.

One of Brian's early sea-going duties was being employed as a deckhand on a millionaire's 'super yacht' giving him another taste of the high life, just as he was about to embark on his own climb to the top. Within fifteen years, he had enough money to purchase a penthouse which overlooked Carnaby Street in London's Soho district. This world-famous thoroughfare still retained the atmosphere of the Swinging Sixties that Brian had embraced with a passion, as well as enjoying hundreds of passionate embraces along the way!

This trendy location was the perfect base for Brian's many trips up to the capital for business and more pleasure as this prestige address certainly added to the pulling power that impressed the 'dolly birds' as they were then called. They were even more impressed when entering the apartment, as well as sipping drinks on the terraced balcony, overlooking the busy streets as the bright young things went about their clothes shopping in the trendy boutiques. Dedicated followers of fashion were still very much the vogue, in the words of the 1966 Kinks' hit record, but these days the street caters mainly for tourists from all over the world and is a shadow of its former self.

Better part of this story was the person that sold Brian this much sought after property. He was the very same millionaire whose own yacht decks had been scrubbed by this young New Zealander just a few years before! He has fond memories of his time in London, often looking back at the photos he took whilst engaged in business deals, mixed with the delights that Soho has always offered. You can only imagine the fun he had, by looking at these images that show one of the most famous addresses in the world, as well as being part of British history. Modern visitors still throng Carnaby Street with its quaint shops and side streets, offering a taste of what it was like back in the heyday when the capital of the UK became the capital for part of that innovative decade. Britannia did rule the waves yet again, but only for a short while.

Carnaby Street apartment

Carnaby Street penthouse balcony view

Brian later sold this prestigious property for £375,000, so one can only imagine the mind-boggling price that it would fetch these days.

The property market can also be a big gamble, but Kiwi always bought and sold at the right times with his many dealings over the decades.

Carnaby Street from the penthouse roof

Unlike many wealthy people, Brian was, and is a very down to earth guy who has mixed with everybody from low to high levels of society. From a rough dockside pub to the first class salon of the liners, luxury hotels or rubbing shoulders with the rich and famous, Brian just adapts and enjoys the wide mix of the people that he comes into contact with, proving that variety is the spice of life. He certainly led a life of variety as far as the ladies were concerned, remembering one of his early sayings *"So many women-so little time!"*

He never forgets where he came from, as well as remembering the saying *"Be nice to the people on your way up–you might meet them again on your way down"* His social skills and outgoing personality have been at the root of his incredible successes, along with a canny eye for opportunities and gambles, but there are occasions when the cards don't always turn up trumps as you will soon find out.

The Silhouette ran a strict membership policy, especially when it came to the minimum legal age requirements of 25 years for entering a casino. This did not deter a local 18 year old Marc Della Ganna, who did look a bit older in 1974, so tried his luck as rules have always been made to be broken. Marc smiled as he looked back at that time of his life:

"Kiwi had a reputation for running a tight ship. The gambling tables were upstairs and the club was the best place to go in Southampton. I saw many celebrities there and in particular I remember Alex Higgins who danced with my girlfriend one night. I went there most Saturdays until I moved away from Southampton. I never saw Brian again until 1995, over twenty years later. It was quite by chance that I saw the club owner strolling along the marina at Costa del Sol's classy Puerto Banus. He didn't recognise me at first, as my grinning from ear to ear whilst shaking his hand and introducing myself took him by surprise. As we two chatted in the warm sunshine, I explained to him the reasons for my knowing him.

We are good friends. Whenever I visit the Costa del Sol I give him a heads up before I arrive. He always makes me welcome! Brian makes a lasting impression on all who meet him. This positive impact is due entirely to his personality. Whether the meeting was brief or, as in my case lasted over many years with long interludes, you simply didn't forget Brian Kiwi Adamson!"

'Opportunity Knocks' was a popular TV talent show that produced many future household names, with some of the acts being booked as star cabaret into the Silhouette Club. Brian has kept many of the local press adverts that helped to bring fans of that show to the Silhouette, with one of them reproduced here.

SILHOUETTE CLUB RESTAURANT and CASINO

4/5 St. Michael's Square
Southampton
RESERVATIONS:
Tel. Southampton 28135 and 21048

For a complete Evening's Entertainment
ALL UNDER THE ONE ROOF. Open every night of the week for Dancing from 9 p.m. until 2 a.m. Restaurant open from 7.30 p.m.

CABARET
Return of the fabulous

FREELANDERS
of radio and "Opportunity Knocks" for one week commencing Sunday, October 19 until Saturday 25

TWO Shows on Friday and Saturday
First at 9.30 p.m.; second 11.45 p.m.

OUR NEW RESIDENT QUARTET
commences Saturday, October 25

Members c./charge 5/- after 10 p.m. (no c./charge before) Guests c./charge 7/6 — 10/- Saturday evening.
Featuring: **FRENCH ROULETTE, BLACKJACK, CHUCK-A-LUCK** and **AMERICAN DICE** in the Casino.
Application for membership, write or call:
Gentlemen £3/3/0. Ladies £1/1/0. Double £4/4/0.
Temporary membership available for visitors.
NO ADMITTANCE AFTER 11.45 p.m.

Please have consideration for neighbours when leaving the club late at night, slamming car doors, etc.

Southampton group- 'Misty' on Silhouette stairs.

John Bendall (Johnny Baker) of 'Misty' recalls those years:

"I read your 2014 'Kiwi' webpage on Brian Adamson with great interest . There are several pictures on your other pages which highlighted different bands that were resident at the Silhouette. Club. The main featured bands were Gerry Gurr , Neil Hibberd and myself

101

with various others. Not sure how long we were there for but must have been 12 months or so. We used to do many nights on and off, supporting the star cabaret acts, as well as our own show. It was a great place to work. I remember one night the bass player Steve Holegate was a dep, and the bouncer wouldn't let him in because he was too scruffy - had to get Kiwi to persuade him to come back in after he threatened he was going home!

I had an aunt who was Italian, who worked as the cloakroom receptionist, taking hats and coats upstairs. She hung over the balcony upstairs, looking down onto the stage and dance floor, then wave at us every chance she got. I remember many musicians at the club with us including Dave Fulford (ex White Plains) plus George on keyboards, Tina on vocals. Brian wasn't very forthcoming when it came to speaking on the mike, but he made an exception on our last night before we left to work in Thailand to thank us and wish us good luck. Happy happy memories,"

Opportunity also knocked for Kiwi with the arrival of two massive US aircraft carriers, anchored in Southampton Water, as the port has welcomed many American Navy vessels over many years. One of these leviathans was the gigantic USS Guadalcanal berthed on the 30th September 1976, for a ten day stopover, which coincided with a celebrity visit to the Silhouette Club by the current Miss United Kingdom. Nineteen year old Carol Jean Grant was on a nationwide publicity tour around Great Britain, falling in love with the best club in town, as well as being enamoured by the owner, who was in a relationship at that time, so who knows what may have happened in different circumstances?

The old sea dog then cannily printed out a load of free VIP passes that made their way out to the officers on both vessels, inviting them to partake of the hospitality in St Michaels Square. Once again, the club was rammed with good looking sailors, surrounded by the local girls who swooned over these handsome visitors. This recalled the old saying about the Yanks who came over during the war years, much to the consternation of local lads who could not compete with these friendly invaders, who were helping the country out. The same mantra was rolled out again with: *"Over-sexed, over-paid and over here!"* It was a record take at the bars and gaming tables, resulting in the club staying open well past its usual time as the party just carried on and on. Kiwi recalled one of the regular girls who never missed any of these nights *"She used to wear American knickers-one Yank and they were off!"*

Brian with Miss United Kingdom 1976

This gesture was appreciated then reciprocated with an invitation to come aboard one of the aircraft carriers the very next day. Brian and his beauty queen were piped aboard, with a navy band playing them onto the massive lower deck that could accommodate a few football pitches. As one can imagine, the crew were delighted to see this gorgeous young lady, plus envying her proud escort, but having no idea that they were looking at a former sailor who had once sailed the very same seas. There were many more stunts throughout this decade, as Kiwi thought up ingenious ways to keep the Silhouette profile in the public eye, which guaranteed a healthy turnover. By now, Brian had clocked up even more air and sea miles, criss-crossing the world in the manner to which he had become accustomed.

He recalls an off the cuff remark made, when he came face to face with Hollywood sex symbol in Las Vegas, following a luxury cruise to Hawaii and Los Angeles. Often interviewed by any local press, when he landed in whichever city, Brian had not been that impressed by Raquel Welch, whose skimpy fur-trimmed bikini in the 1966 movie 'One Million Years BC' had raised many male temperatures, not to mention their appendages! His comments were widely reported in the media, as he thought she was "average" and he had "seen better looking women on the streets of Southampton!" However, he preferred the natural beauty of the gorgeous Hawaiian girls with their long hair cascading down to their grass skirts, when visiting the islands on the way to mainland USA. He quips *"Wish I had taken a lawnmower ashore..."* It was only a tongue in cheek remark but it certainly made a few headlines, as it was always part of his game.

George Sewell-old shipmate!

Many household names frequented the plush Silhouette Club in its heyday, including a good mate of Brian's, who had worked alongside him in the Merchant Navy. 'Tough Guy' actor George Sewell had also been employed as a steward for the Cunard Line, out of Southampton, keeping in touch with Kiwi since they had both left the ships. London-born George then discovered acting, leading to several much acclaimed film and television roles that kept him busy right up to his death in 2007, aged 82.

Yet another beauty queen with actress Dora Bryan

In between Brian's busy lifestyle, he made time to enjoy himself, jetting off across the globe to visit the top class nightspots. Las Vegas was naturally the main attraction for any playboy/gambler, with the likes of Caesars Palace, MGM Grand and other establishments vying for the attention of the big players in town. Quite often, Kiwi had an open invitation, whereby he enjoyed an all-expenses trip out from the UK, to take his place at the card tables. Flights, plus luxury hotel rooms were supplied to the VIP guests on the casinos special lists, hoping that they might recoup some - or more of the outlay, as the players hit the tables with varying degrees of luck. Kiwi modestly claims that he was not a 'high roller' as such, preferring to quit any game when ahead, unlike many who could not resist further bets, or chasing them when the cards didn't go their way.

He laughs at the memory of one such visit to Caesars Palace in 1977, due to someone making a mistake in the casino accounts office. Upon his return to Southampton, he had checked his bank account, noticing a discrepancy over his bill for the duration of his trip. They had deducted the cost of his room, food and beverages, despite being a regular invited guest. A quick phone call led to a profuse apology for the misunderstanding, along with letter that outlined the refund! Brian had an ongoing account with Caesars over many years, often boosted by some healthy wins in the casino.

It's all part of how the big establishments offer complimentary travel and hotel accommodation, as the top gamblers form part of the 'entertainment'. Onlookers watch the big boys – and girls on the card or roulette tables, as they wager small and large sums. This then serves as an incentive for others to try their luck, but lacking the skills used by the professionals. The house rarely loses, along with the big profits from the 24 hour slot machines that formpart of the whole experiences. Many of us enjoy a little flutter, so what better place than amongst the lights, glitz and glamour of Las Vegas? Not forgetting the lack of any clocks in these premises…..

Kiwi was soon invited back on a regular basis, especially by the Caesars manager, who made sure that he was booked into the luxury hotel rooms, along with first class flights and much more!

> 3570 LAS VEGAS BOULEVARD, SOUTH
> LAS VEGAS, NEVADA 89109
> AREA CODE 702-734-7110
>
> February 25, 1977
>
> Mr. Brian Adamson
> Silhouette Club
> 4/5 St. Michaels Square
> Southampton, England
>
> Dear Brian:
>
> Due to an error at the time of your check-out, you were charged for your entire account during your recent stay at Caesars Palace. As you were to have been our guest for complimentary room, food and beverage, we are crediting your account in the amount of $589.96 and charging for your incidentals only amounting to $191.34.
>
> I apologize for this slip-up and for any inconvenience caused you. With best wishes and regards, I remain
>
> Sincerely yours,
>
> CAESARS PALACE
>
> William S. Weinberger
> President
>
> WSW/rb

Brian was more than enamoured to meet up with Frank Sinatra on a couple of occasions, sat next to each at a baccarat table. As soon as 'Ol' Blue Eyes' heard Kiwi's accent, he started chatting away with him, having a great fondness for New Zealand. Frank mentioned that he had many friends who also loved that beautiful part of the world.

The superstar crooner was known for being 'awkward' with some people, but he connected with this gregarious Kiwi straight away. The lyrics of 'My Way' certainly fit the life story of Brian Adamson - just take a look at the words. The 1979 Christmas and New Year festivities rolled by, but there were big problems looming on the horizon during the later years, due to other peoples' faults, and by no fault of our genial entrepreneur.

Chapter 12 SEVENTIES SCANDAL!

'Scandal' was the name of the 1989 movie, telling the 1960s story of 'good time girl' Christine Keeler's involvement with politicians that brought down the Tory government. Another minor scandal saw Brian ending up in court, following an innocent sexual dalliance with a couple of attractive young girls. He had invested in property, purchasing houses which were then turned into rental apartments, as well as a sixteen room hotel in the suburb of Portswood, just a couple of miles away from the Silhouette club. Brian had his own private penthouse at the hotel, often used as a 'love nest' in a quiet part of the city, as befitted any eligible randy bachelor.

In 1975, the forty year old Kiwi took a fancy to a buxom young waitress, we shall call S, so he telephoned the restaurant where she worked to see if she wanted some fun. She decided to invite her pal L, which resulted in a few drinks at the Silhouette, followed by a short trip up to the hotel, with more booze and laughs as the evening warmed up. All three had donned bathrobes, intending to use the private sauna, but S had apparently felt unwell, so just laid down on a sofa as the other two worked up a sweat. Brian and L then swanned off into a bedroom, for some 'heavy petting' as it was called, but no more.

He then got off the bed, to turn off the sauna, but on his return he saw both girls getting dressed rather quickly, as they 'wanted to go home', so the night ended there as they both left, disappearing into the night. Brian then discovered that some £350 (£2,000 today) was missing from the back pocket of his trousers hanging over a chair, then immediately called the police, as he had a clear conscience over the whole matter. The case went to court, with a packed press and public gallery hanging on every word as S took the stand, in order to explain what had happened on the night in question.

Luckily for Brian, she had pleaded guilty to the charge, thus saving him any embarrassment, although he had done nothing wrong, apart from looking forward to a threesome with two attractive women! He was a single man, so had nothing to hide from anyone, as well as the ladies being more than willing to join him for the night out, supping expensive drinks at the best club in town.

S told the court that she had drunk too much wine, then falling asleep on the sofa, as the other two carried on with the frolics in the other room. She then falsely claimed that she woke up to find Brian 'groping' her, but he was actually busy on the bed with her pal in the next room. S then used the opportunity to steal the wedge of tenners, as well as claiming to be "repulsed at the thought of being used for his sexual pleasures". This raised much laughter around the court, as most knew of Brian's well known status as far as any woman was concerned. She also claimed that she would not have gone to the hotel, if she had been sober, nor have stolen the money for the same reason, but the prosecution dismissed all of her testimony, finding her guilty of the theft.

The defence solicitor had also used mitigating circumstances, with regard to S wishing to 'punish' Brian for wanting to take advantage of her and her mate. It transpired that there had been a minor dispute between Brian and her father-a builder who had done some work at the same hotel, so maybe this pushed her to seek more revenge? She was fined £30 (£180) followed by the indignity of seeing the case reported in the local press, with one of the headlines reading 'Mr Red Blood took two girls to his flat' which prompted a few laughs amongst Kiwi's circle of friends and passers-by in the street, who knew all about his libertine status.

Brian was relieved, as well as being thoroughly vindicated, but would have liked to tell his side of the fiasco in court, as it did leave a nasty taste in the mouth. He felt that it made him out be a 'sex monster' which was far from the truth as he has never forced himself on any woman, but many of these sexual encounters run the risk of false claims, especially where a rich man is part of the story. A reporter later interviewed S at her home, where she merely offered a few words of regret over the sordid escapade that turned sour.

"I behaved stupidly. I had far too much to drink, and when I recovered the next day I expect I would have come to my senses and taken the money back if the police had not come the next day"

News (Screws) Of The World!

Not exactly the kind of publicity that Brian had wished for, but it was soon forgotten, then just put it down to experience, but keeping a close eye on his pockets on future dalliances. It had provided a few laughs around Southampton but 'Mr Red Blood' took it all in good humour as the story soon became 'yesterday's newspapers' in which to wrap up the fish and chips. It certainly made him very wary of any future escapades that often result when certain females take advantage of wealthy businessmen, but it did not curtail his healthy appetite for the opposite sex.

Kiwi's fleet of cars outside the hotel.

Chapter 13 THE EIGHTIES

The next decade saw mixed fortunes for many people, as they were labelled the 'boom and bust years' in which money became 'God' for some, with our hero heading for a fall near the end of it all. It was also the Thatcher years, so things were looking good as the Silhouette tills kept filling up nicely with a steady clientele of regulars and visitors, keeping the lively club going throughout those turbulent times.

October 1981 saw yet another milestone as Brian threw a big night to celebrate the 21st anniversary of the Flamingo Club opening, with the renamed Silhouette that had followed just three years later in 1963. By now, the casino membership had reached the 8,500 mark, with the downstairs club numbers at 5,000. Ever a one for publicity, his next idea was to splash out on a great advertising campaign which saw the Southampton city buses being plastered in signs, reaching thousands of readers all over the place, turning heads wherever it went. An immediate boost in profits proved that this was a great way to let the world know what was on offer, with many more companies copying the idea after witnessing Brian's perceptive endeavour. This unique idea was later copied by many businesses in the area, but once again- Kiwi led whist others followed!

The Silhouette bus

This was one of many local press reports from that busy time, giving a good overview of the club's success and its incredible owner with the golden touch:

Southampton night spot 'The Silhouette' celebrates its 21st birthday on Monday, and one thing is certain. Owner Brian Adamson will be working away in the background, while the champagne corks are popping. For New Zealand-born Brian describes himself as a 'workaholic'. Mentioning that there are times when he works a 15-hour day, he adds "I survive on stress!"

Brian started in business in three upstairs rooms in St Michaels Square, Southampton, after a spell at sea. "In the early days I was my own barman, doorman and cleaner. As I made profits, I also made improvements". That first club was called the Flamingo, but the transition to the Silhouette of today was a gradual process over several years, when the premises were closed for a year for building improvements.

A typical day for Brian begins between 10 and 11am. Much of the daytime is spent with business interviews and appointments. The evening is for socializing with guests and personalities who visit the club – as well as being on hand to deal with any problems. Often the day ends at 4am. But in his mind now are plans to pass on more responsibility to his managers and ease up a little. "I like to travel as much as I can and have been round the world a few times" he says. He is a regular visitor to the United States of America and has often been invited to stay as a guest at some of the top Las Vegas hotels and casinos.

Improving the style and the service at the Silhouette is his plan for the immediate future. And then?....perhaps a club and restaurant in some sunnier clime.

The last sentence was quite prophetic, as this dream came true within a very short time, as did many of Brian's dreams from a very young age. Other dreams can turn into nightmares, as Kiwi experienced toward the end of the eighties, with the idea of semi-retirement crossing his mind. He was also mixing business with pleasure, taking many trips across the Atlantic to enjoy the sights and sounds of America, especially those of Las Vegas. This 1984 photo shows a very lucrative visit on one of his many VIP visits, and one recalls the old joke about this incredible city: Las Vegas is where money talks - it says "*Bye Bye...*" but not in this playboy's case!

One of many wins-$9,800 (over $29,000 in today's money)

By now, Southampton's highest roller was making a name for himself in the gambling centre of the world, as well as grabbing more space in the local Hampshire press, which served as more great marketing and publicity for the Silhouette casino. He worked hard, but also enjoyed playing hard on his various trips to overseas destinations, with wine, women and song providing relief in between the serious gambling. He was now fully established as an international playboy, which saw him rubbing shoulders with a wide variety of A-list Hollywood celebrities, the music business and other moguls who were fascinated by his rags to riches story. Here are just a few of Brian's massive collection of personal photos from across many years, which bring back many happy memories as he looks back on the last few decades.

Joan Collins

Ann-Margret

Burt Reynolds

Bo Derek- she gave Brian a "10"!

Tom Selleck and Mohammed Ali

Champion boxers

Brian has fond memories of meeting his idol on a couple of occasions, in the Bahamas and Las Vegas. He recalls that he had been a

VIP guest at one of the champ's major title fights, as well as having a backstage pass to meet his idol. The two boxers got on very well, with Ali chatting away in a friendly manner, and very down to earth. He was a great talker as everybody knew – very intelligent and funny, so this was another highlight of Brian's star-studded life.

Some of these photos were taken at what was to be Ali's last fight in 1981, when the controversial 'Drama in the Bahamas' fight was staged. There were many problems with the whole event, as the thirty nine year old Ali faced the much younger Trevor Burbick, managing to go the full ten round distance, but losing on points.

With Jackie Stewart – both living lives in the fast lane!

The mid Eighties saw another celebration back in St Michaels Square, followed by a downturn in Brian's life, but through no fault of his own as you will soon learn.

Chapter 14 THE EIGHTIES-UPS AND DOWNS

Brian was riding even higher throughout this time, with his well-established status as a very successful gambler who had gained a place on the A-list at Caesars Palace, with regular invites plus all expenses paid. Gamesmen, and women from all over the world had standing invitations from the Casino, with a line of credit opened in the names of the trusted players. His favourite game was Baccarat, in which he maintained a steady 80% winning level, which is much higher than average. Years of playing, watching and studying the game-play saw him bet, then cashing in his chips at the right time, as well as attracting an audience of onlookers that boosted the atmosphere in any casino. His strict rule was to avoid any alcohol when at the table, despite a never ending stream of free drinks on the house, as he kept a clear cool head for hours at a time.

Sadly, Kiwi broke this rule on one fateful occasion, whilst attending a three day junket at the prestigious Desert Inn back in Las Vegas. In return for first class airfares, hotels and full expenses, these specially invited gamblers are used as clever marketing tools, in order to tempt others to have a flutter in the casinos, spurred on by the 'big boys'. These professional gamblers are expected to spend a certain amount of time and money at the table, which inspires onlookers to try their own luck, but often losing much more than they expected. It's all show-business.

By day three, our own playboy was up by $60,000, so feeling pretty confident but with a degree of complacency kicking in. Brian then upped his stakes with $10,000 bets at regular intervals, which saw a mass of people crowding round for a better look at this game. For once, his luck ran out, which saw the end of this session losing him $240,000. Brian stood up, shrugged his shoulders and sauntered off in his usual casual cool manner, vowing to make up for this massive loss on the next time around.

In between his other USA visits, he recalls an amazing invitation in July 1985, as a VIP guest of Dolores Owens-a major name in the gambling world. This executive had started out from her own humble origins in Michigan, before making her way down to Las Vegas in the late Seventies, where she first worked as a lowly pit clerk, then a secretary. She then rose through the ranks, until attaining high positions with Caesars Palace as casino host. In later years she also served as executive vice president for MGM Mirage Middle East and European marketing, so quite a big noise in the industry. She got on very well with Brian, both being self-made successes in life, which led to the invitation sent across the ocean, landing on Brian's desk at the Silhouette Club. This was a star-studded dinner event, to celebrate the lady's tenth anniversary with Caesars World International, with a very privileged guest list, so quite an occasion.

> **CAESARS WORLD INTERNATIONAL**
>
> Dear Friends of Caesars:
>
> The staging of Special Events, whether it be for champions or amateurs, is a fact for which Caesars is well known throughout the world.
>
> At this time we are making plans for an event to honor one of our own champions. We, at Caesars World International, want to share in this very special event.
>
> On July the 27th, 1985, we will be staging a special dinner party, honoring DOLORES OWENS, Executive Vice President of our Middle East Operations. This occasion will mark her tenth year anniversary with Caesars. We feel honored and privileged in counting her as a member of our management team and we want to extend our thanks and appreciation for her accomplishments, loyalty and devotion to Caesars and to you, our most important customers.
>
> We extend a cordial invitation for you to be our guest for this special occasion. It will be held at our Caesars Atlantic City Resort where we have just recently completed a $190,000,000 expansion. It is a fabulous resort, with every possible amenity, and we look forward to having you as our guest to enjoy an exciting visit. We have many wonderful surprises in store for you.
>
> You will be accorded the full VIP services. For those of you arriving in New York via London or Paris, we will arrange for your Concorde airline tickets. It is just a short flight from there to our Caesars Atlantic City and we will have our private jet, helicopters and limousines at your service.
>
> We sincerely hope that you will plan your schedule to be with us on July the 27th. I know that DOLORES will be delighted to hear from you and to offer every assistance with your plans.
>
> Please let us hear from you soon. We extend our very best wishes and warmest regards to you and yours.
>
> Sincerely,
> CAESARS WORLD INTERNATIONAL
>
> J. Terrence Lanni
> President
>
> JTL/cmw
>
> *I would be greatly honored by your presence.*
> *Dolores*

Although Brian had the chance of flying over by Concorde within a few hours, he preferred the genteel route by sea, which offered a more relaxing few days on the QE2 out of Southampton. He was accompanied by his then current girlfriend Sheila, who later became his wife. So - even more of a grand time to be savoured before landing in New York Harbour, where a waiting limo drove them to a nearby helicopter strip, followed by a scenic flight to Atlantic City, further down the East coast. The theme was Ancient Rome, with appropriate togas being worn by the guests.

Dolores Owens and special consort!

The couple had another terrific star-studded night, meeting up with a few more celebrities along with fellow gamblers, enjoying one of the finest parties ever seen in Atlantic City. He also bumped into another legendary boxing manager, who was then mentoring a promising new young boxer by the name of Mike Tyson, so the talk naturally gravitated towards the noble art. They both laughed at the memory of a previous encounter when Kiwi and Tyson met on the steps of a private jet at Las Vegas airport. One of the entourage grabbed a few photos, but later discovered that the film had not wound on properly, thus losing more memories for Brian's scrapbook.

Brian and Sheila

Carry on Cleo!

Says it all…..

    To round off this memorable visit, Brian naturally played his cards right yet again, walking off with one of many big cheques that have boosted his healthy bank account over many years. $44,000 which was worth about $104,000 in today's money.

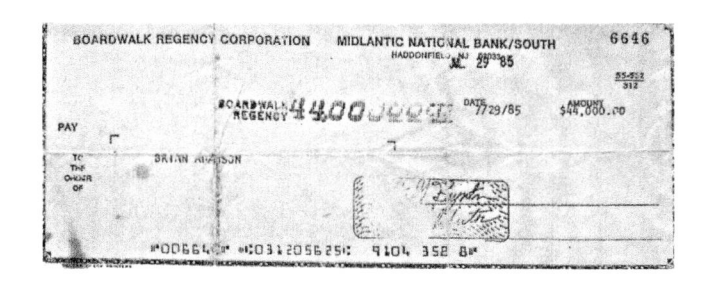

This was just one of many such trips through this manic decade, giving Kiwi ideas about the possibility of retiring from his own club and business interests as it was now coming up to another anniversary bash at the Silhouette. A quarter of a century had whizzed by, since his small Flamingo club had blossomed into the incredible success of the Silhouette, leading to preparations for the next big night out. Invitations were printed out, as everybody geared up in readiness for yet another party that would be talked about long after the October festivities.

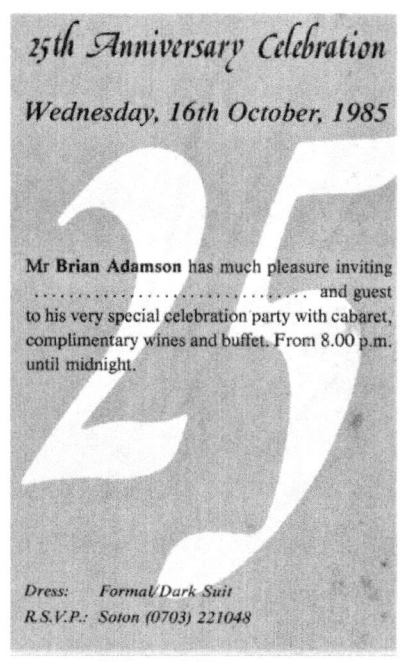

Silver Silhouette

Twenty five years had flown by, as Brian looked back over the quarter of a century that saw his early gambles lead to riches beyond his expectations. He and his loyal staff had been working around the clock, but Brian was enjoying the jet-set life as the invitations kept coming in at regular intervals. One of these being a 20th anniversary week organised by Resorts International Casino, based in the Bahamas. The location for this latest challenge was in Lake Tahoe, California, with some 75 odd top gamblers taking part in a highly competitive baccarat competition. Brian grabbed second place, which resulted in $9,500 being paid in to his account, causing a few more laughs as he strolled away from the tables, quipping *"I should have done better…"* Caesars Palace held him in such high esteem, with even more all-expenses trips out to Nevada, as well as being awarded the use of the corporation yacht, as it cruised on Lake Mead in neighbouring Arizona. This also offered the chance of a helicopter trip along the nearby Grand Canyon, in between hot lazy days as he sunbathed on the deck, surrounded by a posse of pussy, before enjoying more pleasure below decks, but not washing the plates this time round.

"So many women - so little time…"

As you can imagine, Brian had never lost his love of the sea, which gravitated toward another historic milestone that saw him book another first class voyage on the much-loved QE2 which had graced her home port of Southampton since 1969. Captain Bob Arnott was one of the most celebrated captains, who had steered this, and other magnificent Cunard liners across the world's oceans for some forty years, but he was now due to retire with one last turn at the helm. He was more than pleased to welcome the familiar face of our own former merchant seaman-turned millionaire playboy. Brian was invited to the captain's table, which was a common occurrence whenever any skipper learned about the background of this very special passenger, as well as finding him great company. Bob was actually born in Australia, so had a tenuous link with Kiwi, as well as meeting each other on several crossings to New York and elsewhere. Brian recalls long conversations with the captain, much to the chagrin of fellow passengers who clamoured around, in an effort to have their own chat, plus numerous photo opportunities with the ship's master.

Old Sea Salts

Again, the thought of retirement was swimming through Brian's head, as he was now in his mid-fifties which is often a turning point in many lives. However, most of us cannot afford to give up work, unlike those who accrue a fortune, giving them a chance to spend the latter years along whichever path of life they choose. His love life had been a roller coaster ride, with many rides under his belt over many years, enjoying the company of some beautiful women. Long and short term girlfriends had been and gone, plus loads of one-night stands and quickies in all kinds of places, but his status as one of the most eligible bachelors was about to change.

Back at the Silhouette, all was going well, as Brian kept up the pace with more publicity stunts, top entertainment and a first class reputation. The atmosphere was never the same whenever he was away from the club, as he made a point of talking to everybody. He also promoted boxing events around the town, which drew even more customers as well as attracting sponsorship from local businesses, not forgetting the glamorous girls who strutted their stuff around the ring in between bouts. The current climate has now seen a major downturn in any area of entertainment, in which these attractive ladies are featured, thanks to the PC brigade that highlights any minor transgression.

Kiwi's Kuties

Silhouette dancers

During these boom years, the club saw a never-ending succession of celebrities and VIPs who visited the best place in town, including a much respected couple of Southampton councillors, who both later became Mayor. Jack Candy passed away in January 2018 at the grand age of 95, and Brian remembers the many great nights when Jack and wife Irene attended many official functions as well as many off-duty evenings when they let their hair down!

The Silhouette helped to raise many thousands of pounds for local causes across the many years, as many charities can testify, with this great photo that shows M.C. Alan Reynard handing envelopes to Irene, with a glimpse of the white tuxedo sleeve as the 'Boss' was just out of this shot.

Mayor Irene Candy on a fund-raising night

A personal souvenir for Kiwi

Longleat Trip - Kiwi

Yet another great day out for Fairfield Lodge Childrens' Home, as Brian organised a coach trip to Longleat House Safari Park and stately home. He also gave each child a present as you can see in the photograph above, with Kiwi in the front row just before the excited young passengers left Southampton for the journey. This was just one of many such trips that the Silhouette Club kindly promoted and still remembered to this day.

The late Eighties were about to become a turning point in Brian's colourful life, on a personal and business level. The club was going strong, as Kiwi was enjoying his many trips around the world, safe in the knowledge that the venue was in the capable hands of Ann Palmer alongside Raz the casino manager. 1987 was another pivotal year, as the Gaming Board was getting even stricter about granting, or renewing the licences for casinos across the country, which saw many lesser clubs closing down for good. Great news for the Silhouette, as this was only one of two local casinos that were given clean bills of health, allowing them to carry on trading.

Yet another Mayor in a spin

Any casino runs the risk of being caught out by a big win, which had to be covered by all clubs lodging a £1m bond as security for this possibility. On top of that, all gambling establishments had to keep a close eye on any suspicious game play at any table, as the pickings were very rich for any criminal activity. It is common knowledge that bent croupiers can collude with their seemingly innocent players, but having a well-rehearsed system at play.

New York was another of Brian's favourite cities, being the city 'that never sleeps' sung by Frank Sinatra, who often sat alongside him at the same gaming tables over in Las Vegas. It also gave him a chance to visit Wall Street, meeting with various businessmen in this famous thoroughfare in the middle of the financial district. Sometimes on official business, Brian had contemplated some investments in the USA, as well as mixing socially in local bars or at high society gatherings. All the time he was carefully checking out the way in some companies work, as well as looking at the stock market, but preferred to leave his gambling in the casinos. Often a safer option, when one considers the fragile state of any large economy that can see catastrophic falls in share prices.

Another confidence trick sees highly rehearsed punters counting the cards as they are dealt, collected and placed back in the shoe, again possibly in cahoots with the croupier. In those days, the casinos did not have such high-tech surveillance cameras, often relying on well trained staff that walked around the tables, keeping a watch out for anything out of the ordinary. Brian knew all of the tricks, as well as his efficient staff, so there had never been any incidents that could result in negative publicity for the much-respected Silhouette. He would soon be making the biggest decision ever, as he weighed up the choices of working his nuts off, or maybe it was time to cut and run?

Chapter 15 END OF AN ERA

Kiwi recounts his feelings at that time of his life as he was starting to get fed up, having attained many of his early aims in business. He had been working hard as each of his enterprises came to fruition, but felt that the time was right to sell up and enjoy the fruits of his labours over the advancing years on the horizon. Brian was proud of his past life, having made an impact as well as making a lot of money, which is meant to be enjoyed at some stage. He had turned 50, wanting to avoid a mid-life crisis, so carefully considered the many options. Other reasons for getting out of the club game had been due to his many battles with the local council, as petty bureaucracy caused headaches with their licensing department. 1982 saw the Tall Ships Races visiting the city, with various events around the waterside area. Naturally, our former sailor was keen to capitalise on this high profile week, apart from his love of the sea and all that goes with it.

Kiwi put forward a proposal to fill St Michael's Square with tables, chairs and side stalls in the style of a French open-air day. The planning department accepted it, but then hopes were dashed by the licensing side of the council as they refused the sale of alcohol. This was based on objections from certain officials as well as from local residents in nearby Bugle Street, who feared 'unruly behaviour and noise levels'. The Silhouette was plagued by these same complaints across the years, due to a minority of late night revellers who ignored polite advice from the door staff as they left the premises in the early hours. However, Brian contested these ill-founded reasons, as nearby pubs and restaurants saw their own customers parking all over same area, with the inevitable late night disruption.

Further restrictions were then made by the council to limit the festivities to the afternoon period from 3-30 to 6-00, leading to Brian scrapping the idea. The introduction of parking meters in the quiet square had affected the daytime trade for the Kiwi Restaurant in the early years, followed by the proliferation of yellow lines on the adjacent roads. This then caused more problems for club-goers on the evening trade, so all adding to Brian's frustrations.

> ## Plush Silhouette Club is about to be sold!
>
> NIGHTCLUB owner Brian Adamson — one of the richest men in Southampton — is selling his plush Silhouette Club in a deal rumoured to be worth millions. And he is leaving Southampton Council with the parting gift of legal action.
>
> Mr Adamson — who has run the St Michael's Square club for 27 years — claims the council have not supported his enterprise.
>
> "I have served two writs on the council because of the way they have closed the square to parking, reducing access to the club," said Mr Adamson.
>
> "I have enjoyed being a nightclub owner but after nearly 30 years I want more time to travel abroad," said Mr Adamson who still has several business interests in the city.
>
> He said another difficulty was in getting staff. Although the wages he offered were above the going rate some workers with families found they could get more money on the dole.
>
> "I have seen many clubs come and go in the city but this will in some way be the end of an era," he said.

By the mid-Eighties Brian had finally decided his future, as well as celebrating the birth of a daughter, following a short-lived relationship and marriage, so the time seemed right to sell up. Several companies had expressed an interest in buying him out in the past, but he was very careful about such a major move. Leading Leisure was the South's fastest growing company during these times, headed by Roger Gilley and Barry Malizia. They seemed to have the 'golden touch' and, after many high-powered meetings, the magic figure of £3m (£8m today) was agreed on. Not bad for a little business that grew from a £300 investment back in 1960, that had now elevated the impresario into multi-millionaire status.

Around that time, he remembers sitting next to David Sullivan on one of the many flights out to Las Vegas, as they talked about their various business interests. Sullivan had made his fortune out of soft-porn publications, followed by X-rated dating magazines that offered much more than a cosy night out at a restaurant! His later dalliances saw him publishing the 'Daily Sport & Sunday Sport' tabloids, whose contents shocked the more conservative types, overshadowed the much-maligned 'Sun' newspaper.

1982 saw David Sullivan convicted of living off immoral earnings, but after a successful appeal he was released after serving 71 days in prison. Sullivan explained that he did not feel embarrassed about the initial source of his early fortunes. *"I've made a lot of people happy. If I was an arms manufacturer or a cigarette manufacturer, and my products killed millions of my clients, I'd have a bit of doubt about the whole thing. I was a freedom fighter. I believe in the right of adults to make their own decisions."*

David later sold his newspaper holdings for some £40m in 2007, but still retained his other dealings with West Ham FC as a major shareholder. His philanthropic side has seen him donate a lot of money to good causes, so who are we to cast stones? Sex sells as a much-needed commodity with a steady supply and demand over the last few thousand years. Sex had been a major part in Brian's life, but things were about to change, when meeting yet another beautiful woman in London. He was 'married' to his beloved Silhouette club, although he had been contemplating an ordinary side of life, by settling down with a real family. One of his stock quips at that time was *"Why get married and make one woman unhappy, when you can stay single and make them all happy?"* Things changed quickly in 1987 when his pretty girlfriend told him that a "little Kiwi" was on the way. Being the perfect gentleman, Brian felt under obligation to relinquish his bachelor status, which amazed everybody who knew him across his skirt-chasing years.

Kiwi felt that Leading Leisure was on a roll, with a good track record and potential growth, so he negotiated a split deal. He took £2m in cash, as well as taking £1.2m in the company shares, which looked like providing him with more income in the near future. High interest rates, general recession and bad investments by these two whizz-kids soon resulted in a massive downturn over the next couple of years. This saw the share prices drop through the floor, leaving Brian with a massive loss that was spiralling out of control. Leading Leisure had apparently ploughed a lot of money into the Isle of Wight, just across the Solent, causing Brian to question the wisdom of investing in an area that was only operating through the main summer season.

Goodbye to the Silhouette

The boom soon turned to bust for the once proud Leading Leisure, whose empire had turned to dust, which left many shareholders with their own losses. Brian was genuinely saddened by the thought of so many ordinary people losing out, but this is yet another side of gambling that doesn't always pay off. At least he had banked a sizeable fortune, in readiness for the next few years, so put it all down to experience with no obvious sign of regrets. Kiwi has always been positive in everything he has done in life, comparing it with playing for high stakes in casinos all over the planet.

> **INVITATION**
>
> Monday, 28th September between 9.30p.m. and
> 1a.m. in the Silhouette Nightclub
>
> ## Brian's Farewell Party
>
> and to celebrate the birth on 14th September, 1987
> of ARIANNE TASHA ADAMSON
> to Brian and Sheila
>
> R.S.V.P. Tel (0703) 227859   (strictly by invitation only)

The final party

The time had come to say farewell to the dreams that came true for out intrepid club owner, as well as a double celebration party with the birth of their daughter. Many tears were shed on that last night inside the Silhouette, as members, friends and staff said their last goodbyes. The local Echo had published many articles on Brian's incredible progress since first setting feet on our shores back in the late Fifties. Often fed little snippets by the canny club-owner himself, leading to more publicity for whatever venture was being planned. However, they were not aware on another big news story that broke just a few days before, as wedding invitations had landed on doormats across the city! The most eligible bachelor in town was settling down with his long term girlfriend!

The news came as a massive shock to everybody who knew of the most famous playboy in town, with the local press soon finding out that Kiwi's wings were now about to be clipped! An article appeared in the Southampton Echo a few days before Brian stood at the altar, as his beautiful bride and six month daughter Arianne entered the church to seal the knot, witnessed by a packed congregation of family, friends, staff and many more onlookers. I have copied the text in order to let you read the piece that is too small by its reproduction on the page.

Courtesy Southampton Echo (The Bargate Diary)

Could the rumours be true about Southampton's most eligible bachelor, millionaire Brian Adamson, getting married? Indeed they are. "Yes, I'm settling down at last" said the 53-year old New Zealander, who on Saturday marries Sheila Francis, 23, at St. Michael's Church, Southampton, only yards from his former Silhouette Club which he sold last year in a £3m deal. Ironically, the wedding reception won't be held at the Silhouette, now controlled by the massive Leading Leisure empire, for a very good reason. "I'm barred from the club" said Brian. "I don't know why. I've never been given a reason. Anyway, it's not the club it used to be, although I have no quarrel with the directors of Leading Leisure." A Leading Leisure spokesman declined to comment on Brian's claim.

Brian, who still maintains a £1m financial stake in the leisure company has, as he admits, more personal matters on his mind right now. His bride-to-

be, who is from Mauritius, did in fact do the proposing. "Well – it is Leap year, isn't it?" said the former ship's steward. The couple met at a party in London, and have a six month old daughter Arianne. "She's absolutely beautiful, like her mother" says the doting father, who for years rejoiced in the title of Southampton's oldest teenager. They have no immediate plans for a honeymoon because the groom is still the workaholic he's always been, and high on his priorities is the supervision of his new business venture in the Spanish resort of Marbella, where he's building a massive restaurant called the Silhouette. You can't keep a good man down, it seems.

Brian is also having a villa built nearby, but he's still maintaining his business links in Southampton which include a hotel with a penthouse suite, where he is currently up to his eyes in wedding preparations. "I haven't seen Sheila's dress, but she says it's magnificent and I know it will be".

I can reveal that fellow Sotonian Bob Sperring will host a lavish reception for the couple on Saturday, but they have no immediate plans, apart from their Spanish venture, for a honeymoon. The word is that though Brian will be unable to resist the opportunity to show off his young bride to New Zealand folks at the earliest opportunity.

The marriage took place at St. Michaels Church, on the 26th March 1988 at 3pm, with wonderful memories of a great day. Good friend Bob Sperring kindly offered the use of his large house in Chilworth for the lavish reception, following some disagreement with the Silhouette Club's new owners next door. Bob being part of the very successful Sperring family whose chain of newsagents has been established for many years.

Our Wedding

Bride Sheila Francis.
Groom Brian Adamson.

Were United in Marriage on

March 26th. 1988 at 3·00 p.m.

Officiated by

Maid of Honour

Bridesmaids **Jessie.**
Matron of Honour **Christine**
Chief Bridesmaid **Julie**
Flower Girls

Soloist

Ceremony at St. Michael's Church, St. Michaels Square, Southampton
Best Man **Paul Asher**
Ushers

Organist

Photographer **David Bampton.** LMPA.LBIPP

Brian quipped "Signing my life away…"

The couple had already been blessed with a baby daughter, that thrilled him to pieces as a new husband and father in the early stages, but it all sadly deteriorated within a couple of years. It was no surprise to his friends and colleagues, when he told them that he had made a big mistake in his chequered life, so was contemplating a quick exit from this doomed marriage. Within a year, the couple ended up in the divorce court, with Brian's natural concerns over how much this was all going to cost him, as the wife and any children are generally the winners in these sad stories. Brian winces at the memory of the outcome, as Mrs Adamson was awarded the couples' two bed apartment in upmarket St John's Wood on the outskirts of Regents Park, close to Lord's Cricket Ground. A near neighbour being Paul McCartney, who had purchased his town house back in the Sixties, located a short distance from the legendary Abbey Road recording studio.

He remains on good terms with Sheila and Arianne, without bearing any grudges or regrets, as it's all part of the rich tapestry of life. They enjoyed their last times together out in Marbella as Brian had planned to open up a new venue, which attracted the rich and famous who flocked to the New Silhouette in Puerto Banus.

By 1990 the situation was so bad that Kiwi sold off 100,000 shares for a measly £1500, but kept the others back in readiness for another piece of media coverage that filled the front pages of local newspapers, before escaping to his Australian holiday home for the winter in the sun.

I've lost a million – ex-nightclub boss

FORMER nightclub boss Brian Adamson burned his 'worthless' shares in a Southampton leisure company – outside the charred remains of the Silhouette club he used to own.

The hotspot was bought from Mr Adamson in 1987 by the South's fastest growing leisure company Leading Leisure headed by Roger Gilley and Barry Malizia.

At the same time, he invested more than £1.2 million in Leading Leisure's shares.

But the value of shares in the company crashed. This year he managed to sell off 100,000 for just £1,500.

"They ran before they could walk," said Mr Adamson.

"They were buying things that weren't making any money. They bought half the Isle of Wight – for what? Three months a year of business."

Wheel of fortune turns sour for the man who sold his casino

● BEFORE the number came up... Roger Gilley, (left), Brian Adamson and Barry Malizia, (right).

Summoning his usual media contacts, the press descended on St Michaels Square yet again, to witness Brian holding the remaining worthless shares aloft. The cameras clicked as Kiwi ceremoniously set light to what was once worth over a million pounds. Ironically, more flames were in evidence within a couple of years, as the Silhouette complex was gutted by a 'mystery' blaze that raised many local eyebrows. After renovating the burnt out premises, it was re-launched as the Curzon Club, finally being taken over by the Stanley group of casinos. Later years saw the whole building turned into private accommodation with an office complex on the corner, but the mock Tudor frontage has remained, overlooking the front entrance of the church.

Although the Silhouette Club is long gone, the memory will never die as Brian brought a new landmark to the city that is still talked about to this day. Many Southampton nostalgia-led Facebook pages, plus other social media outlets still mention the 'best club in Town' as they recall the heady days that brought that area to life. It is part of our modern heritage, and will be talked about for a very long time to come.

The combination of this marital strife and his unexpected loss over the Leading Leisure wrongdoings might have led to depression for most of us, but Kiwi has always been a fighter and survivor. It's all part of life's ups and downs, as he wistfully reminisces in the latter part of a rollercoaster story that he wanted to share with the world. Dusting himself down, it was time for the next stage in his quest for more fun in the sun, and back on the singles market as he cast his eye over more ladies who crossed his path.

Chapter 16 CARRY ON UP THE MED!

Brian had sailed in and out of Southampton over the past thirty odd years, from lowly beginnings to savouring first class status on the world's finest luxury liners, but now he was preparing to leave our shores forever. By this time, our playboy had been buying, selling and renting out property as well as having his own sea-going yacht berthed in the nearby harbour. This was his second maritime toy that he used on many occasions around the Solent or across to France and beyond. She went by the name of 'No Harassment' which raised a smile whenever sailing by, and soon led to more amusement when being implicated in a criminal investigation in Spain. Despite the partial loss on the sale of the Silhouette, Brian still had a few million pounds in the bank, but now it was time to make hay while the sun shined, so decided on waving goodbye to his beloved Southampton, heading for the Spanish variety of sun, sea, sand, and sex.

Kiwi was praying that this final voyage would not be a repeat of a previous jaunt that could have echoed the ending of the 1912 Titanic story, as he laughs at yet another episode in his gilded life. Another one of his lines *"Yachts are like women. Yachts are trouble, they are expensive, and the best ones seem to belong to someone else."* This trip saw the vessel crossing the busy Channel to the French port of Cherbourg, before carrying on through the turbulent waters of the Bay of Biscay, which had seen many ships end up at the bottom of the sea, or broken up on the coastal rocks if lucky enough to make land. Although being an experienced seaman, Brian was not qualified to skipper his yacht, so was legally bound to have a ticketed helmsman in charge, although he was able to assist.

They eventually found refuge from the stormy sea in the Spanish port of Corunna, in order to wait until the elements had settled down. Just before the expected departure, Brian and the hungry crew were feeling peckish, as the meal had been delayed for some reason. It then transpired that the randy skipper was having his way with the attractive ship's cook down in the yacht's luxury suite. He was servicing her instead of servicing his vessel, which didn't go down well with 'the Boss' who insisted they set sail at once, foregoing some food. The skipper had also neglected his important duty of checking the weather forecast, daring to challenge Brian on the lines that *"We cannot sail yet without knowing the conditions out there. You're the gambler–I'm not"* Needless to say, Kiwi exploded with heated words between the two, which in previous centuries might have seen the miscreant walk the plank. Brian's final words were on the lines of *"You can f**k the cook, but not my yacht!"*

Ignoring the skipper's pleas and warnings, the yacht set sail back into the heaving seas of the unforgiving Atlantic Ocean, which soon became more unsettled as a big storm came blowing in, causing much consternation amongst those on board. The rollers got higher, as the wind picked up, causing the vessel to rock all over the place, as well as giant waves swamping the decks that threatened our anxious sailors who were now in a state of panic. The worst case scenario would see the mast damaged, or the rudder control put of action with disastrous consequences, so it was time for Lady Luck to take over as this gamble had not paid off for once in Brian's life. Unfortunately, the radar equipment had suffered some damage, which was another major worry for everybody, although they were not too far from the safety of the coast. After many scary hours, the weather abated, which then saw the skipper exercising his authority, being wholly responsible for any incidents on the water. Brian had no further say in the matter, as the stricken vessel limped slowly back to the safety of the port of Corunna. Expensive emergency repairs were made, but at least there had been no loss of lives on this fateful trip, and once again Brian thanked someone up there.. Not for the first time in his life that he had cheated death by train, and now by sea albeit via 'No Harassment'….

It was soon time to set sail yet again, as the weather settled down to see the jolly sailors head out towards Lisbon, then onto Gibraltar, to stock up on some duty-free booze before berthing in the harbour at Puerto Banus, near Marbella, next to some of the biggest super yachts in the world. He kept the yacht moored there for a couple of years, but did not use it as much as he had hoped, apart from a few trips across to Ibiza and other lively islands. The novelty was wearing off, as well as the spiralling high costs when pitching up in this premium area. This led to Brian using his craft to sell his own craft at fairly good price, but she soon popped up again in the very near future in a very different light.

The mooring fees in this part of Southern Spain are amongst the most expensive in the world, but not all the yachts are owned by the various millionaires and billionaires who flock to this resort, rubbing shoulders with A-list celebrities. Many vessels are chartered, thus giving the chance to 'ordinary' people to sail around this beautiful part of the Mediterranean, enjoying sunny climes all year round. Many tourists take a break in the surrounding area, but gravitate towards Puerto Banus to soak up the atmosphere of the pretty harbour area.

This photo shows the Adamsons and friends relaxing on their yacht

'No Harassment' Puerto Banus Marina

'No Harrassment' later surfaced as a story across front page news in the local and national Spanish press. Brian nearly dropped his copy of 'Diario Sur' when reading about a massive drug bust in which his former vessel had been impounded, following the discovery of some 475 kilos of hashish in the hold. The Guardia Civil had arrested the crew, who were using the yacht to transport drugs between the usual journey across the Straits of Gibraltar and the Moroccan coast, which has been a well-known smuggling route for centuries. Brian's phone rang off the hook, as the news leaked out, but his friends were more than relieved to learn that he had sold the yacht, having nothing to do with its new use.

El SVA aprehende 475 kilos de hac[hís] [e]n una embarcación de bandera in[glesa]

Spanish press report

So - the label of 'No Harassment' had led to more laughs as everybody talked about this case for a long time after. As it must be said, Brian has always been as clean as the proverbial whistle, always playing fair in every single enterprise and transaction throughout his life. Any casino owner is well aware of the cash that passes over the gaming table, often having an inkling of its source by virtue of knowing who was splashing out, but that was nobody's business but the punter. His was not to question the source of any cash that came fluttering across the gaming tables.

CHAPTER 17   NEW SILHOUETTE IN THE SUN

Although he had sold up everything back in the UK, Brian still missed the good old days when ruling the roost at his precious nightclub, missing the buzz of it all. The wealthy types who flocked to Marbella had plenty of cash burning a hole in their designer pockets, as well as looking for upmarket clubs to spend much of it. No surprise then, when he purchased a property, which then was launched under the same nostalgic name of his beloved English establishment. This soon saw a steady stream of well-heeled guests and more great nights at the newest 'in place' in town.

The Silhouette Puerto Banus

Restaurant view over the harbour

Trade quickly took off, as the outside balcony area offered the perfect view over the sea, plus spectacular sunsets leading to the evening festivities. Ever the perfectionist, Brian had a retractable roof installed, enhancing the whole experience for dining 'al fresco'. Resident DJs, live bands and top line cabaret acts kept the place swinging until the early hours, but Brian had decided not to apply for a gaming licence as the Spanish set-up was far removed from the UK way of operating such premises.

As in the Southampton days, the local Spanish press also filled several pages, with news of the opening, as well as reporting on the various A-list celebrities who graced this plush new club. The lunchtime trade was also keeping the staff busy, with a steady stream of customers from the visiting yachts, as well as passing trade, regulars and many more visitors from all over Europe and beyond.

As before, Brian hired a superb team of staff, keeping a close eye on every aspect of the day to day running. The local Spanish authorities were also very impressed with his new club, not forgetting providing employment and good business for local suppliers.

This photograph shows the lounge bar area as Brian orders his lunch from head waiter Antonio, as well as the three roof sections that slid silently back to offer fresh air for the customers below. Once again, his constructive brain and eye for décor came into play, following on from the Southampton years, not forgetting a lifetime of world travel across the decades. As soon as any yacht moored in the harbour, the seafarers soon found their way to this luxurious new establishment, either as regulars or by asking anyone in the port for the best place to go.

The new Silhouette had no great need for paid advertising, as word of mouth soon ensured a steady stream of visitors, with the attentive Brian welcoming every single customer with the personal touch. He was ecstatic with the resounding success of this new venture, as the venue brought back memories of the old club back in England. The atmosphere was great, offering an international flavour which enhanced the whole experience. Kiwi was also pleased to see old friends and customers from the Southampton club, who often called by when in Marbella.

Brian's pulled again!

One of Brian's regular guests at the new club was another worldwide star, who had also made a break out of her poverty-stricken background as a young girl in Cardiff, so yet another talking point between these two people who shared a common bond of a 'rags to riches' life story. Shirley Bassey asked if she could celebrate her birthday at this classy new venue, along with many of her celebrity friends–real 'big spenders'. You can see how thrilled she was, when being serenaded with 'Happy Birthday' by billionaire Adnan Khashoggi and company in the photo. The Khashoggis had one of the biggest holiday villas in the area, so were regular visitors to this swish venue as well as becoming good friends with the genial host

Bassey Birthday Bash!

Shirley Bassey with Adnan Khashoggi-a real Big Spender!

This extraordinary night carried on till dawn broke over the Mediterranean, being just one of many visits by the jet-set pals who always made a bee-line to the new Silhouette Club. More photos show other well-known guests at the club, which kept the local paparazzi busy by the front entrance.

Shirley Bassey

Brian - the Khashoggis - Sheila

Lionel Blair

Many visiting celebrities were regular visitors to the New Silhouette, just a few yards away from Puerto Banus Harbour as their yachts were moored nearby. Lionel Blair being another famous UK television personality, well known as a choreographer and appearing on many shows since the Sixties. He always made a bee-line to the restaurant, enjoying a great night out with his family and friends, as well as stepping onto the dance floor as he strutted his stuff.

Messrs Adamson &Stringfellow – Playboys inc.

Another regular was fellow playboy club owner Peter Stringfellow, whom Brian had known from his Carnaby Street days. They had enjoyed some crazy nights all over London as you can only imagine, with all of those beautiful women that surrounded the showman. Peter was born some five years after Brian, being the son of a Sheffield steelworker, suffering from the usual post-war difficulties with a less than satisfactory school record, partly due to dyslexia. He left school, to work as a sales assistant in an upmarket gents' tailors, giving him a flair for fashion that exploded during the colourful Sixties. Another good-looking womaniser, who later escaped a dull life to join the Merchant Navy as a trainee waiter. Sounds familiar?

As you can surmise, this pair got on like the proverbial house on fire their lives mirroring each other in so many ways. During the early Sixties, Peter saw an opening for teenage dance halls in his Yorkshire area, which saw him book many up and coming new beat groups, including the fledgling Beatles just as they were breaking into national fame. Later years saw him become one of the top club owners in the country, moving down to London, setting up lap-dancing clubs in the capital, with an open VIP invitation for his good pal Kiwi. Again, this gave Brian a few ideas that later resulted in him investing in 'adult entertainment over in Spain a few years later, as you will later read about.

David Hasselhoff & Adamsons - Marbella

Telly 'Kojak' Savalas- "Who Loves Ya Kiwi!

Rod Stewart is another popular visitor to Puerto Banus, often stopping to chat with fans as they spot him along the harbour, as well as posing for photos and 'selfies' with no attitude, unlike some celebrities. Brian met him on several occasions in the local 'watering holes', sharing anecdotes plus many laughs as you can imagine.

Frank Bruno

Frank Bruno - one of the U.K.s favourite boxers, who held the WBC champion spot for a short while, before facing Mike Tyson. As you can imagine, Brian enjoyed swapping stories about their respective fights and colourful lives in and out of the ring. He has fond memories of this popular celebrity who always called by whenever back in Puerto Banus.

Chapter 18 THE NAUGHTY NINETIES

Southampton had a special place in Brian's heart, but now it was time to settle down in the sun, but not too far from the UK, as he still retained business interests plus old acquaintances from those wonderful years. Marbella has long been one of the most popular Spanish destinations for the wealthier types, who spend vacation time there, or buy holiday homes as a place to get away from it all. This suited Kiwi, although he was not considering any retirement plans as yet, with plenty of energy and the will to keep busy.

He has so many memories, that could possibly fill another book to carry on from this one, but picks out certain stories that should be shared, hence the reason for this very publication. Brian had met Victor Lownes on many occasions, including several trips to the world famous Playboy Club on Park Lane, opposite Hyde Park in one of the most expensive parts of Mayfair. Victor was Hugh Hefner's right hand man in the UK, running the London club, which boasted the most beautiful 'bunny girls'. Many of these glamorous models had been spread across the pages of the Playboy magazine, as well as being spread across Hefner's bed back in the Playboy mansion. Victor called Brian up, as he was in Marbella for a few days, so naturally invited him to a private villa nearby, in a very secluded area, which provided many celebrities a much–needed degree of privacy.

Once again, Kiwi mixed and mingled with the assorted millionaires, television and movie stars, but was less than impressed with one certain actor. George Hamilton was more famous for his perma-tanned face, than any of his appearances on the small and silver screens over many years, as well as being well known for his narcissistic persona. Brian took an instant dislike to Hamilton, who was swanning around the rooms, telling all and sundry about himself, which hardy impressed anyone at all, judging by the way that onlookers soon made excuses to go for a drink, or chat with someone else in the next room.

The night then took a turn, as a few selected guests were driven down to the harbour to board a super yacht, belonging to one of Victor's friends, a Russian billionaire who was celebrating his birthday. Amongst the guests were Australian rock star Michael Hutchence, lead singer with INXS, which neatly summed up his lifestyle, much of it in excess. He was accompanied by his latest girlfriend, who had made a name for herself as a feisty television presenter on various music shows. Paula Yates had recently split from her husband Bob Geldof of the Boomtown Rats/Band Aid fame, being attracted to the wilder side of life with the controversial leather-clad stud whose sexual exploits were well documented.

Brian's Antipodean connection kicked in, as they all chatted away for ages about their combined interests. He noticed Paula's bump and offered to donate 50 Euros towards her baby fund, as was the custom, to add to a new account set up, in order to save money that would be accessible on the child's sixteenth birthday. She later gave birth to her second daughter, by Geldof, naming the little girl as Peaches. Sadly it all went terribly wrong as Michael died in strange circumstances in 1990, followed by Paula's passing in 1996.

July 1995 saw the death of yet another one of Brian's good friends – a colourful character whose exploits over many years had filled the Spanish press as they reported on his many exploits. Don Jaime de Mora y Aragon, a flamboyant Spanish aristocrat whose amiable antics had made him the toast of the Costa del Sol, died at a hospital near his home in Marbella, Spain. He was 70 with his obituary being published in newspapers all over the world, including the prestigious New York Times. This followed a series of heart problems in recent years, thus ending another amazing life story that is still talked about all over Spain to this day. The son of a wealthy count and a member of a collateral line of the Spanish royal family, Mr. de Mora was born in Madrid in 1925, but soon dropped out of this aristocratic life to enjoy the fun side of life, as he settled in Marbella in the early 1960s.

Brian's Christmas card from the Zurbano Palace Madrid

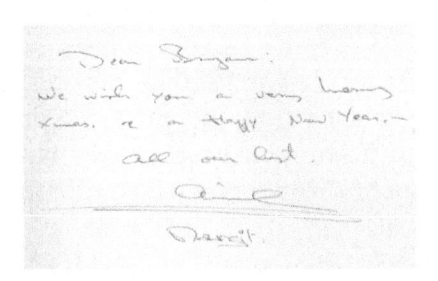

"Dear Brian – We wish you a Very Happy Xmas and a Happy New Year. All our best – Don Jaime and Margit"

His popularity grew around Marbella, amongst the wealthy and well-connected as the resort was attracting the rich and famous from all over the world. The city's Tourist Office also made him its official 'greeter' with his looks and personality to the fore. He struck an imposing figure, with his tall slender body, slicked-back hair, waxed moustache, monocle and walking cane as he strolled around the harbour and town. Some likened him to a regal blue-blooded Salvador Dali, another Spanish hero, which amused him greatly..

Don Jaime was mainly a promoter, as a well-known figurehead for various business ventures, including nightclubs as well as theatrical productions and other show-business outlets. However, these were all financed with other peoples' money, including his own annual parties with help from billionaire Adnan Khashoggi. Kiwi has many fond memories of his good pal, often pausing by the statue of Don Jaime in Marbella, as he recalls the great fun days of yesteryear. Jimmy was married to the beautiful Margit Ohlson, and the couple were regular guests at Brian's New Silhouette Club, causing a stir whenever they appeared at the door.

Statue of Don Jaime de Mora y Aragon, Marbella

SCENIC AIRLINES

FLIGHT CERTIFICATE

This is to certify that

MR BRIAN S. ADAMSON

is a member of that elite and highly selective group that has flown through the Grand Canyon with Scenic Airlines, and, as such has viewed scenery beyond description and is an expert on the geological history of Planet Earth.

2/16/91
DATE AWARDED

John R Seibold
PRESIDENT

High flying Kiwi!

Once again, Brian took another trip along the Grand Canyon, as he had done back in the Eighties which really was a decade of ups and downs. The next ten years were also filled with many more journeys, combining his usual love of business and pleasure, with even more ladies sharing the fun. Even more 'canyons' were navigated, with the added safety net that saw Kiwi having had the 'snip' in order to avoid any repeats of his former mistakes, as you will recall.

He was also often invited to Universal Studios in Los Angeles, bumping into many top Hollywood names such as Robert Stack, the star of several big movies. One of his biggest successes was playing the lead character of Eliot Ness, in the award-winning television series 'The Untouchables' back in the early Sixties, which was also popular in the UK. This classic show was set in the Prohibition era, as the federal agents kept up their relentless battle against the Chicago gangs.

Brian had enjoyed spending money on cars, but was never flash enough to pose around in a Ferrari, Lamborghini or a Bentley, but had his favourites over the years. Some of his stable have included a Mercedes 450SL, plus a rare Italian ISO Grifo, which currently sell at around the £350,000 mark for an average model, with higher prices for certain ones. His big love was a Mercedes 500 SL drop-head, which he purchased in 1989, being the perfect car for driving around the sun-soaked parts of Southern Spain.

Puerto Banus Harbour

It certainly turned a few heads, especially those of the ladies, who sometimes later 'gave head' in the front seat, when parked on a hill overlooking the Mediterranean! Five years later, he bought the much sought-after registration plate BA 1 for some £4,800 (nearly £7,000 these days) that he had been after for a long time. These number plates have proved to be very lucrative investments over the years, as Kiwi knew after several offers were made by various people who were keen to have this cherished plate on their own vehicle.

Sure enough, the time came when this iconic number was ready to be sold off, with an eye-watering £130,000 being paid for the transfer, but Brian kept the car for another few years until having it shipped back to the UK, to be sold off at a classic car auction. Sadly, this beautiful machine only sold for a few thousand, as it needed quite a bit of work to bring it back to its former glory. It had been re-sprayed in gold, as befits the owner, but was previously a gorgeous black colour.

Brian Adamson – the One!

Golden Girl

Sadly, the rare 1960s Iso Grifo met with a sticky end, as you can see by this photo below, which shows a hairy moustachioed Brian saying goodbye to her.

Iso - Ouch!

As the New Silhouette had closed for a while, following a downturn in profits, due to the economic climate, Brian then decided to emulate his old pal Peter Stringfellow, setting about with plans to open a 'Gentlemens' Club'. It was open to the (escorted) ladies as well, with strict house rules that offered a degree of sophistication–not always found in some establishments of this type, so he looked forward to this fresh start that soon grabbed the attention of the Marbella elite. Firstly opened as the Camel Club, later changing to Las Chicas, as the venue gained a good reputation on the Costa del Sol, albeit with the usual detractors who frown on any business based on this industry, but sex sells!

As per Brian's usual flair for publicity, this new attraction needed something special for the launch night, as the local press were in attendance. Kiwi hired a real camel led by a gorgeous girl, who was naturally dressed in flimsy see-through 'Arab' clothes. However, this was one young lady that he didn't manage to 'hump'....

This new enterprise took off, being very successful on the financial side, as well as providing the chance for the 'Boss' to interview the deluge of gorgeous young ladies, who were looking to earn very good money in a safe environment. The auditions must have been fun, as Brian needed to vet all applicants, to make sure that Las Chicas offered classy girls, unlike many inferior establishments. He has always run a tight ship, ensuring that no negative publicity be allowed to besmirch his good name.

Sadly, there are some of these particular clubs that fall well below the acceptable standards, as well as attracting unscrupulous women who have their own agendas. In August 1998, one local Spanish newspaper featured a story that was concerned with complaints by dancers, who had been promised a wonderful job in the sun. They looked forward to good wages, apartments and all that goes with any holiday destination. It went to court, as it was alleged that some of the girls were shocked to discover that their 'duties' were expected to be of a very different nature than merely dancing on stages.

Once again, lurid accounts of being lured into unsavoury working conditions led to one headline of 'How Dancers Became Trapped In A Web Of Vice' which implicated Las Chicas, plus two other venues. It transpired that two girls had been working in three clubs around the Marbella area, but alleged that two of the venues were 'no more than brothels', therefore implicating Brian's club by association. As one can imagine, Brian was furious at this slur, immediately instructing his lawyer to instigate proceedings against the tabloid and clear his good name.

The newspaper admitted full liability for this careless example of poor journalism, followed by a printed apology to the effect that a false impression had been created by the article. The women also claimed 'mistreatment by Brian Adamson' but these were also proven to be false allegations. It reminded Kiwi of that episode back in Southampton during the Seventies, when taking two ladies back to his own private penthouse, with a promise of a threesome. That ended with one of the ladies stealing a massive wedge of banknotes from the back pocket of his trousers, hanging on a chair before disappearing into the night with the loot.

The newspaper's own lawyer made a full apology in court, as well as underlining Brian's excellent reputation for professional behaviour. They accepted full liability, in addition to paying out the equivalent of £20,000 in damages plus his full legal costs, but the whole matter cast a shadow over this area of entertainment. Although the Las Chicas profile was not directly affected by this publicity, Brian was considering the possibility of selling up as the economic downturn was still at the same level.

Kiwi was a born gambler, continuing to grace the tables all over the planet throughout the years, with being labelled a 'hit and run' player. Quite simply meaning that he has always quit when ahead, leading to a high 80% success rate, which most gamblers can only dream of. It is far too easy to be tempted into chasing any losses, by continuing to keep on betting 'just in case'. Gamblers also risk being impaired by alcohol, which Brian always avoided, as a rule. He was playing seven-card stud poker at the Barracuda Club in London, with another well-known gambler Max Thomas, a Cypriot bookmaker. Brian was showing a pair of Kings, whilst his opponent only had a small pair on one hand. Kiwi then boldly placed £25,000 into the pot that was already showing £50,000 in bets, before Max looked across the table, looking for any hints across Brian's face, before calling him.

Max held two pairs against Brian's Kings, so had called his bluff before raking the chips over to his considerable pile. Kiwi's reaction? A shrug of the shoulders, then those two words *"Shit happens...."* Stud poker played by a stud has a certain ring to it. It was time to bid farewell to the Nineties, as the New Millennium was about to usher in yet another cycle of this incredible life story, with Brian taking more time to relax and enjoy spending much of his wealth.

Chapter 19 PHUKET!

1999 saw this former dishwasher-turned millionaire club owner reach the pensionable age of 65, but this guy was far from the slippers and pipe brigade, as you can well imagine. His property portfolio was spread across several countries, which suited him just right, having itchy feet which saw him hopping on planes, spending time in each location. As the 2000s crept in, Brian kept up his jet-set way of life, with never a dull moment, combining more business deals with making the most of his enviable social life.

Kiwi was a survivor in so many ways, as you will have read about his near-misses over many years, but the biggest one was yet to come along. It was early morning on Boxing Day 2004 as Brian was spending some time in Phuket Thailand, lying in bed with Kai, his (then) current girlfriend. Andaman Beach is one of the most sought-after locations in Asia, as he knew very well from many visits over the years, leading to the purchase of this prime real estate. Kiwi owned a triplex penthouse suite located on the top three floors of the finest apartment block in the area. Sipping cool drinks on the balcony, with glorious sunsets over the ocean have remained in Brian's memory ever since. A real taste of paradise, but the constant travelling was a major factor in letting it ago, and he was not getting any younger.

The earth had moved for the couple during the hot steamy night, but little did they know that a real undersea earthquake out in the depths of the Indian Ocean unleashed one of the worst natural disasters in recent years. It was a high tide in this part of the country, being one of the main tourist areas, which was a contributing factor as the ensuing tsunami gathered up its deadly force, sweeping across a large swathe of the Asian seas and oceans.

Some 250,000 or more people lost their lives, homes and much more in the path of these gigantic shock waves that led to major floods in all coastal areas in some fourteen countries. The tired couple could hear some commotion from around the apartments, as well as looking out of the window to see the streets packed with people in some kind of panic. He turned the radio on, to find that the channels had been taken over by the news programmes, warning of a terrible storm on the way, as well as advising people to find safe refuge.

Many people reported their bed shaking in the night, but one can only guess that it was not noticed in the high penthouse as Kiwi banged away in his well-honed manner. The names of Phuket and Bangkok have always led to obvious word play in this part of the world, but this was no laughing matter during this festive time.

The building started to shake, which prompted the couple to get dressed, then running down the stairwell, avoiding the lift in case of being trapped, as the area had experienced earthquakes in the past. They hit the streets which were full of panic-stricken locals and tourists, all clamouring to find out where to go, as conflicting reports were coming in from all directions. Some headed towards a nearby community centre, which saw Brian and his Thai girlfriend join the throng, as at least she could translate what was going on.

The screaming intensified as the centre became packed with scared people, but it soon became apparent that any ground floor level was not the best place to be, in the path of possible flooding from the ocean. Many of these people then started to run out of the building, so it was decision time for the worried couple, as Brian dragged his girl away, making their way back to the apartment block to return to the top floor of the well-built structure, which made sense for their safety.

They could not believe their eyes as they rushed to the window, then out to the balcony to gaze across the ocean that had suddenly been enveloped in darkness as the black storm clouds gathered above the water.

The normally calm waters were churning as never before, and they could see a massive wave rushing toward the shore, as if the end of the world was on its way. The tsunami hit the beaches, with millions of gallons of filthy seawater crashing over the roads and buildings on its death-laden path of destruction that saw cars, buses, boats and any loose items that were swept away, carried inland to wreak more havoc. Trees were uprooted with power lines crashing down on the streets below, with sparks flying out as they made contact with anything on the ground. Restaurants and shops disappeared along with the rest of the coastal road that had taken the first impact of this phenomenal force of nature that claimed many lives in the immediate area. The couple saw the waters racing across the ground below them, as the massive tidal wave covered the tennis courts below, as well as flooding the underground garages. The lower apartments were also swamped by the seawater, as it carried on with deadly force to the inland areas as well.

When the waters eventually subsided, an eerie calm came creeping in, as survivors ventured out to salvage what they could, from broken homes and businesses, as well as trying to trace their relatives, friends and neighbours who had gone missing. The smell of death lingered in the tropical heat of the day as the emergency services did their best, working around the clock to try and bring some order back to the devastated area. Brian and a local pal took a walk along the nearby Patong Beach that was now unrecognisable, in the wake of this hell-driven deluge. Many boats that had been previously been bobbing up and down in the quiet harbour had now ended up a good mile inland, being swept along like toys. His local supermarket had borne the brunt of the waves, with its occupants crushed beneath the collapsed roof of its flimsy building, as well as the community centre that had suffered the same fate. Many more had tragically drowned, as they had been trapped in underground areas, seeking shelter from the storm. Once again, Brian was a survivor, as he counted his blessings once more, but there was more to come....

With advancing age, Kiwi was looking to wind down his property portfolio, being more settled in Marbella, as the Costa del Sol offered him all that he really needed. In 2013, he decided to put his Phuket penthouse on the market, with the following sales information published in Thailand and across the world. The marked arrow on the photograph shows the top floor apartments, located in the finest part of the whole island, where Brian enjoyed all that this piece of paradise could offer. He stayed there whenever he had the time, especially during the recent years, enjoying the company of his local girlfriend and the great social life, plus many trips to local tourist spots.

"UNIQUE PENTHOUSE FREEHOLD. 540 M2 OVER 3 FLOORS.

Considered to be the largest and best penthouse on Phuket Island in the best location. 5 minutes walk to beach. 15 minutes walk to Patong centre. Nothing can be built in front. Building is 21 stories high. Only 2 penthouses on top. These are the details of this property:

Full use of the Andaman Beach Suite facilities (restaurant, room service, gym, maintenance call-out, laundry service, Wi-Fi, telephone, air-conditioning, hitel swimming pool and sauna. See Andaman Beach Suite website for more details. This penthouse triplex (comprising 3 floors) has an adjoining studio apartment 213 with connecting door to main penthouse with its own entrance. 2 interior parking spaces on the ground floor are included.

Penthouse comprises main bedroom, 2 guest bedrooms, small childrens' room (currently used as a storeroom). Adjoining toilet and shower- shared with 1 guest room. Attic area has a double bedroom and maid room with bed, shower, toilet with own entrance. Initial sale price is 95m Baht (£2.3m)less 3m Baht for buyer to design their own décor. Sold as is with existing contents. Large terrace with pool, with fantastic sea views in front as well as surrounding views to the hills.

Total selling price of 92m Baht (£2.2m) or nearest offer.

Girlfriend Kai on penthouse balcony- a 'silhouette' !

This beautiful photo was taken in November 2004, a few weeks before the serenity was shattered by the unexpected force of nature. Brian laughed, when telling me that the circular part of the pool was actually a Jacuzzi, with some of the warm water jets pointing straight up from the base. This gave added pleasure to the girls who placed themselves in the right position!

CHAPTER 20 MARBELLA

Another year-another trip, as Brian travelled from Goa up to Mumbai, formerly known as Bombay, staying at the five-star Oberoi Trident, one of Asia's best known luxury hotels. This beautiful building hit the headlines in 2009, when ten suicide attackers stormed the holiday resort over the space of a few days, killing around 100 innocent people, before being shot themselves. It hit Brian hard, when he read about this senseless attack, as well as seeing the awful media coverage across the news channels. He remembered a wonderful time there, meeting so many friendly people from all walks of life, and it brought more feelings of being 'lucky' once again, as he had made plans to return to this very same hotel around that time.

2009 also saw Brian meeting up with a Marbella-based property sales executive, who was instructed to find a new property for Brian in the area. Some of the most exclusive apartments were to be found in Las Terrazas, a gated community that offered a wonderful location as well as a high degree of security. The deal was sealed, that saw Kiwi move in for a short while, before his itchy feet saw him back on the move again. Not long after moving in to the much sought after area, Brian felt more inclined to relocate back to Thailand, occupying his classy penthouse triplex suite that offered 360 degree views of Phuket, close to the ocean that had certainly been a cause for concern on that fateful day in 2004. He enjoyed more time in this tropical paradise, but later relocating back to Spain with another visit back to England to catch up with a few old friends.

The Costa del Sol can be too hot for some people during the main summer season, which saw Brian getting back to Southampton for a break, escaping from the sweltering heat, before returning to Marbella. Things took a turn for the worse in late 2014, when he was playing cards at a friend's house, as he suddenly felt very light headed and uneasy. His pal quickly phoned Dr Victoria Chalon, 7his family doctor and friend, who was living nearby. After hearing about Brian's symptoms, she realised that his blood pressure and pulse rates were dropping, indicating a possible serious heart problem.

This necessitated a speedy dash to the local A&E department of the local Quiron Hospital in Marbella, resulting in Kiwi being admitted to the intensive care unit. Victoria's diagnosis and intuition was correct, probably helping to save his life when the doctors discovered irregularities, resulting in having a pacemaker fitted, whilst under a local anaesthetic. Quite a common procedure these days, but very worrying when the patients are in their eighties, as is any surgical intervention.

He was very weak, but once again proving that he was a survivor, slowly getting back on his feet, sticking another two fingers up at the Grim Reaper. The lease on his apartment ran out in July 2014, which then saw Brian move into a local friend's villa. A short time after, Brian's itchy feet and other body parts were missing his Thai girlfriend Kai , so he took off yet again to enjoy the nefarious Phuket-based delights that he had become used to.

Phi-Phi Islands Thailand

By 2015, Brian had sold his Patong Beach penthouse, moving back to the Marbella villa, as well as becoming involved with a real estate market company, which was slowly recovering from its previous downturns. His global properties had now been sold off, as he decided to take things easy for a while, looking back over the last eighty odd years with a view to sharing his story.

The last thing that Brian wanted was any more health worries, but in late 2017 he suffered from a simple fall, when getting out of a car, banging his head on the pavement but worse still, he had broken his hip. Straight back to hospital for a major operation, followed by a few months of inactivity, as he could only hobble about on crutches for some considerable time, but kept on smiling in the face of adversity. 2019 arrived, with the publication of this very book, which I hope you have been enjoying.

Brian 'Kiwi' Adamson has no regrets, having relished every day of his eventful life, despite the bad experiences which are overshadowed by the good ones. He has laughed, loved and gambled in between the hard work which provided those very words, and maybe some of this may rub off onto others. Nothing is impossible, as Kiwi proved, but luck plays a hand in all of our lives – the biggest gamble of all.

Former Silhouette Club Puerto Banus July 2019

Chapter 21 MISCELLANEOUS MEMORIES

Following his divorce, Kiwi had reverted to bachelor status, making up for lost time with the ladies, as well as looking at new ideas, after selling up the Silhouette Club in Puerto Banus. Never one to sit still, he recalls one time when searching for a property on the California coast, chartering a light aircraft to view these palatial beach-side homes. A clever way to check out the neighbouring properties, as well as getting a much clearer idea as opposed to wasting time in the offices of the real estate companies. He retained his Marbella villa, but always on the lookout for other ways to invest part of his considerable fortune as well as enjoying the trips.

Over many years, Brian had ticked off the dream destinations from the time when he spread the old map over his bed, as a teenager back in Upper Hutt. His bucket list had grown into a global odyssey, with so many memories that he often forgets. On one of many flights to Las Vegas, he found himself sitting next to a senior executive from a major television company, based in London and Los Angeles. The two struck up a conversation, which amused the American as Brian entertained him with some of his escapades with the ladies. It then transpired that his fellow traveller was a good pal of Hugh Hefner, which led to being handed a business card, with an invitation to the Playboy mansion the next day. Kiwi was gutted, as he was tied up with a three day baccarat tournament at the MGM casino, so missed out on the opportunity of a sex-laden lifetime. Can you imagine Hefner & Adamson together, surrounded by the Bunny Girls long before the label of rampant rabbit was applied to a vibrator?

Another night-time flight from London to Chicago provided the chance for Brian to qualify for the much talked-about 'Six Mile High' club, as he was delighted to sit next to a very attractive young lady in the first class area of a 747. They talked through the long flight, which soon saw the cabin lights dim, enhancing the atmosphere between these two strangers. Brian's smooth chat soon turned into a sex-charged frisson, leading to exploring fingers underneath the blanket that resulted in a hasty coupling. No flight attendants were walking up and down the aisle, as well as the cabin only having a few other passengers seated well away from the couple, thus providing the perfect opportunity for a quickie in the air.

Kiwi had also added a beautiful waterfront villa to his ever expanding property portfolio, located by Surfer's Paradise in Queensland Australia. He spent a lot of time there, in between renting this luxury bolthole out to those who could afford the high price. Although he was very careful in vetting all prospective tenants, things took a turn for the worse when letting the property out for a year, before the rent payments suddenly stopped. Local businessman Peter Foster and his family enjoyed the delights of this expensive home, before cancelling the bank payments, leading to a hasty eviction via Brian's legal team in the area. Many will recall this name, as Peter Foster has led a life of career criminality all over the world, with money laundering and various get rich schemes that have landed him in jail in many countries. The UK recalls his involvement with former Prime Minister Tony Blair's wife Cherie, as he was involved in buying Bristol based apartments at knock down prices. Another scam saw him teaming up with former page three girl/topless model Samantha Fox, promoting 'Bai Lin Tea', which promised dramatic weight loss-an ancient Chinese method using a secret compound. It was later found to be normal black tea. Samantha had been taken in by the prolific con-man, but kicked him into touch as the whole enterprise went 'tits up' to coin a phrase.

Following 9/11 and other terrorist atrocities, the world has become a much different place these days, as air travel has become a nightmare, with added security measures that cause massive queues at any airport. When Brian was globe-trotting through the Eighties, he often managed to sweet talk his way out of any problems, laughing at the time when he had to fly out to Zurich, in order to arrange some business and banking facilities. He arrived at the Heathrow check-in desk, only to discover that he had forgotten his passport, which would normally have led to losing the flight. The officer checked Brian's documents which validated the reason for this particular journey, along with good-natured chat on both sides.

After double checking that Brian was actually booked on the return flight, he was then waved through the boarding gate, which somewhat confused the relieved traveller. *"Is that it?"* enquired Brian, to which the officer replied *"Not quite, Sir. You will have to present your passport to the immigration desk when landing in Zurich. I hope that they are having a good day like me!"* Fortunately for Brian, this was the case on entering Switzerland, as well as getting back to the UK without further hassle. The Swiss officials were stricter than their UK counterparts, but upon looking over Brian's bank correspondence, hotel reservation and other details, they allowed him to carry on his way, but with mild rebukes for this oversight.

Paris was another favourite place for any red-blooded visitor, within easy reach of the UK, so Brian took full advantage of many trips to another city of sin. He smiles again when recalling an invitation to an imposing chateau on the outskirts of the capital, during a business visit as well as checking out the racy nightlife in the city. Upon arrival, he immediately recognised the owner, who was hosting this lavish function, as a top ranking official in the French government. Discretion being the better part of valour, Brian does not wish to divulge the identity of his genial host, who had laid on an impressive banquet for his distinguished guests from the top realms of French society. The food was of the finest calibre in the French tradition, with the expensive wine flowing freely as most of the guests enjoyed the atmosphere around the massive dining table. As you probably know, Brian has never been a great imbiber of alcohol, especially at the card tables which can often impair judgement, so he drank a moderate amount on this particular night.

In between one of the many courses, a hush fell on the room as a beautiful naked girl waltzed in through one of the large doors, passing by with a wink and hinted invitation to follow her across the hall, leading to another room. This had obviously been pre-planned by the millionaire chateau owner, as he smiled and suggested that everybody should take a little excursion around this mini-palace. The assembled partygoers then left their seats for a guided tour, which revealed many interlinking rooms full of naked writhing bodies in full blown successions of orgies. Copulating couples on the floor, on chairs and sofas as well as across tables provided a spectacle for the amused passers-by, and aroused other guests as they proceeded on their way through this Bacchanalian display of lust. Some took their clothes off, to join in the fun, whilst others quickly turned back, heading for the table to finish off their meal. This brought a whole new meaning to inter-course entertainment, and you may be surprised to learn that Brian was not impressed with this surprise show, as he felt it degraded the act of sex which is normally enjoyed between couples who know each other, albeit for a short time so long as they fancy each other.

He has enjoyed sex with a couple of ladies on many outings, but not with an audience as in this case, feeling that this orgy resembled a meat market, with some of the participants acting like animals. Furthermore, the thought of hidden cameras might leading to scandal in high places crossed his canny brain. The memories of his old pal Diana Dors made him smile, as she had also organised 'adult' parties on the same lines. Legend has it that she kept a secret collection of tapes locked away in her safe, the likes of which could have major repercussions amongst the rich and famous party-goers that attended these raunchy nights.

Another gag: *"Sex between two people is a wonderful thing. Between six people – it's f*****g fantastic!"*

In the time-honoured way of investigative reporters, Brian and his friend made their excuses and left. You may recall the Stanley Kubrick 1999 movie of 'Eyes Wide Shut' as the 'Satanic' orgy scene more or less echoed that very night. However, Brian is not averse to threesomes, as displayed on a free night in Las Vegas, as he hailed a cab, asking the driver where the best action was. The recommendation was for the Barracuda Club, which Brian was happy to accept. Just as they were ready to drive off into the night, Kiwi noticed two ravishing beauties standing by the kerb with looks of dismay on their pretty faces, so he stopped the taxi. They had hoped to grab the same cab, but Brian had just got there a few seconds before, so he gallantly wound the window down to see if they wanted to share the ride.

Coincidentally, they were also bound for the same club, giving Brian the chance to enjoy the ride, and maybe a later ride if things worked out well. After paying the cab fare, with a handsome tip, our Sir Galahad accompanied these two cuties into the Barracuda Club, but lost sight of them as they went off elsewhere, leaving Brian heading for the casino area. Later on, they bumped into each other again, then having a few drinks as they got to know each other. They introduced themselves as a couple of lucky ladies who were enjoying some time off work, having just won a competition from their sales company with an all-expenses paid trip to the glittering city. The mutual attraction hitched up a notch when Brian invited them back to his courtesy suite at Caesars Palace, often inhabited by such stars as Sammy Davis Jr and many more of the A-listers in town.

Top US comedian Alan King in Las Vegas-chatting up Kiwi's latest squeeze!

Caesar's Palace VIP suite

Within a few minutes of the three gigglers entering this plush apartment, Brian was entering one of the girls in the master bedroom, which soon attracted the attention of the other lady who popped her head around the door. Needless to say, this turned her on, leading to a menage-a-trois that lasted long into the night, before room service knocked on the door early next morning. Just one of many wonderful nights, that saw an exhausted playboy go back to bed for a well-earned rest, as the girls bade farewell. No wallet left in back pocket of his trousers, as you may remember a similar tale of woe a few pages back! Once bitten - more than twice shy.

Busy bedrooms above

Since 2001, Brian has taken photos of many young ladies who pass him by, as well as making sure that he knows who they are, as a way of protecting himself from any wrongdoing or possible recrimination by any gold-diggers who have an agenda. The old sailor has literally had a girl in every port, enjoying the pleasures of all nationalities across a lifetime of hedonistic pleasures, maybe numbering some 2,000 or more. If he had made notches on his bedpost, then it would have been sawdust a long time ago, having slept and fornicated in many beds in his fun-packed time. Even on tropical beaches, sofas, car seats, tables and all manner of handy locations provided the perfect opportunity for Brian Adamson, also known as 'Martini' if one recalls the old advertising campaign: *"Anytime-any place- anywhere!"*

Despite advancing years, Kiwi still managed to pull the birds, as he retained his good looks and well-honed chat-up lines that still worked. Another ruse saw him take on a new identity as a 'scout' for a model agency, with a batch of business cards being printed. These were handed out to many a pretty young thing, walking through Puerto Banus and nearby areas, or when passing through Brian's clubs. Like many attractive well-endowed girls, they were often keen to capitalise on their assets, in order to emulate the Page Three stunners who were making big money plus celebrity status, by the simple route of baring their breasts. Howls of protest by the Mary Whitehouse band of sad losers failed to stop the flow of this never ending display of beautiful bodies, which boosted a major part of the economy, by simple supply and demand.

Many were invited back to the villa, to be impressed by the luxury surroundings of this millionaire's home, as well as looking at his collection of valuable paintings on the wall, as opposed to the cliché-laded 'etchings' which was a standing joke phrase a few years ago. Brian morphed into his 'David Bailey' mode, whipping out his camera, and much more after many a steamy photo-shoot that turned both parties on, not forgetting that many of these aspiring models went home with a portfolio of topless glamour photographs that often led to much bigger opportunities. Many of them fell foul of unscrupulous agencies and photographers, and were taken advantage of - such is the way of the world, but not to be condoned. It's all part of life's experiences, and Brian's conscience is clear when looking back over his many conquests, all based on consensual sex that pleasured both sides.

The Philippines have always been a favourite destination for our world travelling playboy, offering many delights of stunning scenery and even more stunning ladies who crossed Brian's path, then across the threshold of his hotel room. He wistfully recalls many memories that shocked a lot of people, when visiting certain clubs and casinos. One such trip took Kiwi and a German pal to the city of Angeles, some fifty miles from the capital Manila, described as 'The City of Sin' as a legacy from the days when US servicemen were 'serviced' by the local prostitutes. The purpose of this outing was to meet up with a guy called Gerard, a very prosperous businessman with a massive portfolio of hotels and many more dealings. The downside of being very wealthy in certain countries is the fear of being kidnapped, which led to Gerard being abducted, followed by demands of $1m for his safe release. Luckily for him, the police were tipped off, leading to a swift raid on the hideout, leaving one of the gang being shot dead, with the others thrown into the local rat-infested jail. Within a short time, these remaining hostage-takers met with unexplained ends in the prison cells, but soon forgotten about. Money talks, with corruption being rife in many countries, so perhaps this retribution was orchestrated? Crime doesn't always pay, especially if the wrong person is targeted.

Gerard invited his guests to his large mansion for a special weekend that filled Kiwi and mate with a sense of anticipation, knowing of their host's reputation. Their car joined a convoy of other vehicles, containing a mini-bus full of pretty young women, winking, waving and blowing kisses across to Brian's car. One un-nerving sight was the presence of an armoured truck, containing uniformed grim-faced bodyguards who were sporting AK47s. This was a precaution, in light of Gerard's vulnerability, following his near-miss on a previous occasion, so no risks were being taken as the group made its way through the jungle roads.

As you can well imagine, this was just another 'day at the office' for Brian and everybody else who enjoyed the delights on offer, but leaving a very exhausted couple of Western visitors plus a few very satisfied local girls. Unlike many other hotspots in the world, the Filipino 'ladies of the night' are genuinely very friendly and accommodating, in contrast to the rather cold conveyor belt route as seen in red light areas. They really enjoy social intercourse on top of sexual side, providing wonderful company for tourists who flock to these destinations. The 'girly' bars are also well run, offering a wide choice of attractive Filipino ladies, with the authorities turning a blind eye, unless any hint of trouble comes along. This is dealt with very quickly, so no wonder that visitors feel quite safe when taking a stroll through the neon-lit streets.

The risk of street crime is a worrying aspect of life, especially in the more notorious parts of the world, which was always in Brian's street-wise mind as he strolled along many a thoroughfare. On two occasions, he let his guard slip as he grimaces when relating the story of having a gold necklace chain ripped from his neck in the Brazilian city of Fortaleza, as the mugger passed by on the back of a motorbike. Two years later, in a similar incident back in the Spanish town of San Pedro, his prized Rolex watch was grabbed as he tussled with another scumbag, who leapt back onto his accomplice's motorbike. On reflection, he realised that this was a foolish reaction as the attackers may have had knives or even guns, so no expensive items are worth losing a life over.

If Brian had kept a diary throughout his fascinating life, I guess it would serve as a template for another volume of memories, in addition to some that have been recorded in this biography. I trust you have enjoyed reading about his exploits and sexploits that have certainly made me laugh as I have been writing about it all. As mentioned before, Brian doesn't do 'regrets', being eternally grateful for a charmed life that very few of us could emulate. He faced each challenge as if it was a teenage boxing match way back in the Fifties, as well as a few near misses that could have cut this story short.

Within a few short years, his new business venture had taken off, providing him with a lifestyle that most of us can only dream of. He also ended up as a first class passenger on several ships, being waited on hand and foot, as many a young lad was washing dishes a few decks down below in a hot sweaty gallery. Never forgetting his roots, this new playboy often recalled how blessed he had been in life, and helped other people along the way, unlike many millionaires who often turn out to be misers! His new found wealth provided the means to enjoy the company of many ladies across the years, but they were treated with respect and the sex was always consensual. Recent high profile news stories have somewhat overshadowed the way in which certain celebrity millionaires have taken advantage of aspiring actresses, or elsewhere in other workplaces. Times have changed, so put aside any prejudices you may have, when having read this story which tells of another era that can be labelled as modern history.

More 'pussy'! A live tiger in Thailand.

MGM Grand Hotel Las Vegas -the actual live lion

The subject of this book is now in his mid-Eighties, living out in Spain in semi-retirement with fond memories of his adopted home of

Southampton, and he just wanted to share his life story. We had made contact a few years ago, with some of the story ending up on one of my web-pages, which attracted a lot of attention from local Hampshire people who recalled the heady days of the nightclub. Former staff, club-goers, friends, business colleagues and many more got in touch with their own memories. Many of them said that it warranted a book, as it would appeal to a much wider audience outside of the city, so here we are!

Brian recalls one time when he owned six properties in the only small private street in Southampton, comprising two houses plus another four that he had converted into flats. Forest View is a small cul-de-sac, just a few hundred yards from St Michael's Square, situated on top of the ancient town walls, close to the city centre. The residents have a wonderful view across Southampton Water. This exclusive street also offers views of the docks and busy shipping channels, including many of the largest cruise ships that carry passengers all over the world, plus the tankers and freight carriers. Brian often stood outside the Forest View houses, raising a smile as he remembered his early days at sea, grafting away below decks, but with a vision of what lay ahead.

Some of these properties were also used as accommodation for a few of the Silhouette staff, as the club was only a two minute walk away, so was much more than an investment. He made an offer to buy the three remaining houses, which could have seen him own the whole street. Sadly, the owner refused to sell, for whatever reason, so curtailing another of Brian's dreams. Throughout his Silhouette years, he had built up a healthy portfolio of properties, which he bought, then sold for good profit, as well as renting them out in between.

Another well-known landmark pub is situated just a short walk from St Michael's Square, the name of which is known to sailors across world. The Juniper Berry had a 'racy' reputation back in the Sixties and Seventies, as visiting seamen, lorry drivers and locals packed the place out. It was a mixed gay/straight establishment featuring live entertainment in the form of drag acts plus the 'open mike' spot. This is where member of the audience would get up on the stage, to belt out off-key songs to the accompaniment of the resident organist. This often led to heckling, banter but all in good fun, this creating a great atmosphere with very little trouble, unlike modern times. When Brian heard that the 'JB' was up for sale, he immediately joined in with the bidding but was not successful on that occasion. His aim was to turn the venue into an upmarket restaurant, linked to his main Silhouette Club down the street.

Other memories have also popped up, as he remembers some great times in Los Angeles, staying at the Beverley Hills Hotel, and driving along Rodeo Drive into Hollywood, where he hung out with a few movie stars, television people and musicians, along with other high-rolling casino players. New York held a special place in his heart, spending a lot of time in the Big Apple, including an invitation to Wall Street where he met some of the top earners in the world, as well as partying with many of them after hours in the top clubs.

Las Vegas was always one of Brian's main destinations, being a regular VIP guest of the main hotels, who kept a close eye on their top-rated players, so often dangled big money carrots in front of them in order to see big money cross over the gaming tables. His favourite places were Caesars Palace, Mirage, Desert Inn and other top hotels/casinos that have become household names. As he always maintains- he has been a 'hit and run' player, leaving the table at the right time, unlike many of his peers who simply hope for better results on the next few hands dealt across the table.

During my 2019 visit to meet Kiwi, I was able to have a look through his vast collection of albums, filled with photos and press reports that chronicled his life's journey. It has been a hard choice to select the images featured in this book, not forgetting that printed paperbacks only publish photos as black & white. The digital e-book version offers the chance to enjoy the original colour of many of the same pictures, at the lower pricing structure of course. It was a mind-boggling experience for me, as I turned each album page, reading more of the details that could possibly lead to a second book. Brian has also kept just a few copies of his winning casino cheques, although he always plays the figures down, maintaining that he has always been a cautious card player. He has never considered himself to be in the 'big league' of the world's leading gamblers, many of whom get hit by massive losses. My eyebrows were certainly raised when noting the figures on the cheques!

As we chatted about stuff, it triggered more memories from hundreds of meetings with the rich and famous. Brian recalls a visit to one of the most exclusive gaming establishments, located in Curzon Street Mayfair, just off Park Lane in London's West End. Crockfords Casino opened in 1828, offering the aristocracy a discreet private club in which to eat, drink and hit the gaming tables. Brian, along with his wife and a lady friend, paid a visit whilst in Town. Sitting at the Baccarat table, Brian recognised the guy sat next to him, as one of the richest men in Australia at that time As soon as this fellow gambler heard Brian's accent, he grinned and introduced himself as Kerry Packer. This billionaire had made his fortune in many businesses, including a newspaper empire plus the major Nine Television network. His most famous venture saw him found World Series Cricket, linked to exclusive television rights all over the world. Unlike Brian, Packer was not a self-made entrepreneur, having been helped by a privileged family background. He was rarely out of the newspapers from the Seventies, gaining notoriety and negative press as a result of his dealings.

Added media attention was due to his legendary gambling in many casinos across the globe, as well as buying into many clubs. One of these being the Crown Casino in Melbourne, one of Kiwi's regular haunts when passing through. Crockfords waived the statutory maximum bet limit for Kerry Packer, as one of the biggest high rollers in the world. This often raised concerns for the house, as Packer had won – but lost millions on many visits to casinos, but he was playing safe on this occasion. He and Brian enjoyed a good chat over drinks, following the card games, with Kerry giving the girls £100 each to have their own little flutter on the roulette table.

The following image shows just three of many cheque copies that Brian has kept, but there were many more scattered across the gambling years as he certainly won much more than he lost. His cautious professional way of playing cards proves that anyone can make a good living in the casinos, although luck plays a big part in the game.

Odd 90/91 wins at Caesars Palace - nearly $100,000 total

Kiwi laughs at another time, when the Mirage Casino invited him over from Spain, complete with all paid travel expenses, along with a luxury villa apartment, plus obligatory swimming pool and all that one expects. He transferred $500,000 from his bank account into the Mirage deposit account, in readiness to hit the Baccarat tables, as he had done fairly well in the past. Cannily, he had no intention of gambling too much of this half million, but tempted by the all-expenses side of the deal.

Viva Las Vegas!

However, a problem came up as soon as our intrepid gambler realised that the casino were now operating 'mini tables', which he avoided at all costs. The main large Baccarat tables suited Brian, so he had no alternative but to pull out of the games, then looked around at another possibility. A quick call to Caesars Palace was met with an enthusiastic invitation by the manager, who booked him into one of the penthouse suites, with standard expenses paid, along with his airfare of some 2,700 Euros. His $500,000 Mirage deposit was immediately credited back to his Marbella bank, leaving Kiwi to get stuck into the Baccarat sessions, that saw him rake up a very good profit, but leaving the game when in front. This is the Golden Rule, which so many gamblers seem to forget, as the temptation of that big win overtakes common sense. It also followed on from the memory of his first ever trip to Las Vegas a few years before, where he joined a high-rolling Baccarat game, betting a risky $10,000 a time The cards and his tactics saw him up by $60,000, then crashing out with a loss of £240,000. This was the only time he ever lost in this city, teaching him a big lesson on when to quit any game. Complacency can often lead to a downfall at the tables, combined with the ever present waitress who serves complimentary alcohol that can impair judgement. Brian made a hard rule to avoid drinking whilst at play, thus keeping his concentration at peak levels - the champagne corks popped when it was all over.

One has to smile at the 'scandal' over certain remarks made by President Trump, that have somewhat dogged his new role as leader of the Free World. The phrase 'grabbing pussy' certainly raised many eyebrows, but many mini-skirts were raised in the pursuit of mutual happiness across the decades throughout the life of Brian! Also, the phrase of *"If you've got it – flaunt it!"* will also underline the basis of this story, and will naturally attract some negativity for some. A common label that is used by some critics to describe this kind of man is a 'dinosaur'. I have made up a new name for him- a Shagasaurus! Others will simply enjoy it and have had a laugh by reading about the antics of a Southampton legend – Brian 'Kiwi' Adamson.

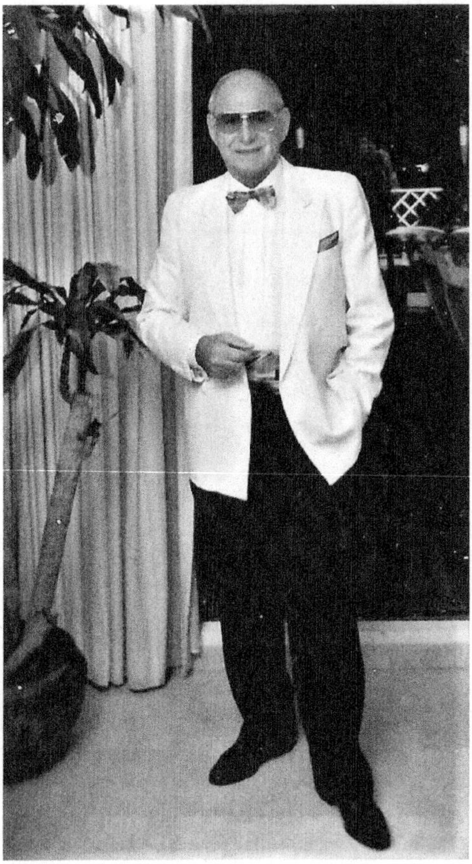

EPILOGUE

January 2020 David St John writes:

I never really knew that much about Kiwi back in the early days, when I was growing up in Southampton, or had any idea of his incredible life journey until he made contact with me in 2014. As he was not getting any younger, Brian had a natural wish to get his story told and to share it with the world - much of which he had visited over the decades. I have had several phone conversations with him, so have got to know more of what makes him tick. He loved his adopted city of Southampton, wishing to be remembered by all the people that he got to know in those exciting times. Fond memories of loyal staff that stayed for many years, as well as the club-goers that flocked to St Michaels Square for the fun-filled nights that often crept into dawn, as the night never stopped. Kiwi looked after those who worked hard, but never suffered fools gladly, which sometimes caused resentment as they were asked to leave.

His mobility has been impaired since his recent accident, but he is getting better as well as paying his usual visits to the local casino. His mind is still sharp enough to play his favourite card game of poker - based 'Texas Hold 'Em' which requires a combination of probability, psychology, game theory, strategy and logic. Kiwi's win/lose ratio is still in his favour, as well as seeing him enjoy the atmosphere and social side of the casino environment that has been part of his life over the last few decades. He naturally misses the buzz of jetting away to another corner of the world, especially the USA trips, and all that went with it as his boyhood daydreams turned into a reality that he could have never realised. Brian hopes that others might manage to do the same as he did, although the world is a much different place these days, as his generation look back on those years.

Women have always been a major part of his incredible life, as it all carries on into Brian's mid-Eighties! He often invites a gorgeous bi-sexual lady - who we will call 'M' - up to his apartment along with her lady friends who provide some nice entertainment for the 'oldest swinger in Town'. Age has not diminished his sexual appetite, so I'm sure that fun and frolics keep him going!

Having had homes across the world, Brian's wander lust has finally wound down ever since he set foot in Marbella many years ago. He is more than happy at settling in Puerto Banus – a piece of Paradise that suits him down to the ground in his twilight years. He quips "I shall stay here until I go to a place where nobody comes back from. Heaven or Hell? I'm already laying bets on it...."

At one stage of Brian's global travels, he took up a temporary residency in Cyprus in January 1990, having fallen in love with the island and its people. This permit still makes Kiwi laugh, as it shows being registered as an 'alien' for the rest of the year. I guess the label suited him over his life, when looking back at some of the many beautiful women who crossed his path – some of them were really 'out of this world'.

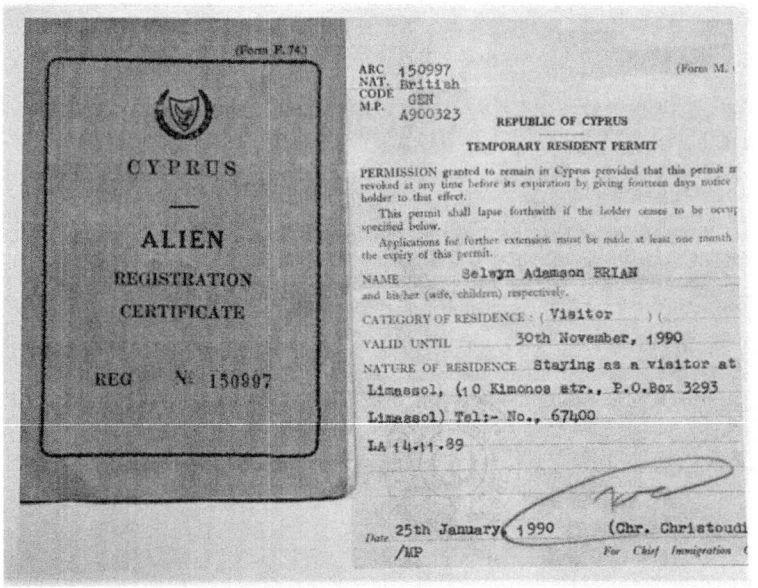

Brian is very philosophical as the years pass by, his will stating that his body will be contributed to medical research, in order to benefit others in the future. Then he will be cremated, explaining; "not wanting worms crawling through my bones in some lonely grave in a foreign land!" His ashes will finally be scattered out at sea – this is where it all started all those years ago when leaving New Zealand on a path that few of us could dream about. In the meantime, Kiwi hopes that you have enjoyed reading about his life journey as this book serves as a legacy to an amazing character.

Brian's extensive collection of personal photos include many great memories of the gorgeous ladies who passed his way, with some of the images not being quite suitable for publication in a book of this nature. He also explains that they form a little bit of 'insurance' in case of possible allegations that may have surrounded his playboy image, as he romped his way through some 2,000 women since the days of the Silhouette Club and across the globe! In addition, I asked if he had any regrets about anything in his star-studded life, or would he have done anything different? In the words of Edith Piaf: *"Non, rien de rien, non, je ne regrette rien...."* His favourite song also reminds him of several meetings with one of the biggest stars of the Twentieth Century, as this massive Frank Sinatra hit also mirrors the life of Brian 'Kiwi' Adamson:

"I did it......My Way...."

FAMOUS NAMES AND PLACES

Artistes who appeared or visited the Silhouette Clubs in Southampton and Marbella include:

THE MOODY BLUES - JUDI DENCH - KEN DODD

CHUCK BERRY - GERRY AND THE PACEMAKERS

ROD STEWART - ACKER BILK - DANNY WILLIAMS

KENNY BALL AND HIS JAZZMEN - DIANA DORS

FREDDIE STARR - PETER STRINGFELLOW AND MANY MORE.

MISCELLANEOUS SPORTS STARS SUCH AS:

MOHAMMED ALI/CASSIUS CLAY - JOE LOUIS

DON KING - MIKE TYSON - FRANK BRUNO

KEVIN KEEGAN - GEORGE BEST - BARRY SHEENE

JACKIE STEWART - SEVERAL SOUTHAMPTON FC PLAYERS AND VISITING TEAMS.

BRIAN ALSO MET UP WITH MANY TV, MOVIE STARS, CORPORATE ICONS AND ENTERTAINERS ALL OVER THE WORLD INCLUDING:

JOAN COLLINS - ANN MARGRET - DAVID HASSELHOFF

BURT REYNOLDS - BO DEREK - TELLY SAVALAS

BRUCE WILLIS - SYLVESTER STALLONE

ROBERT STACK - JACK NICHOLSON - ZSA ZSA GABOR

KERRY PACKER - GEORGE SEWELL - ROSS KEMP

BARBARA WINDSOR - DOLORES OWEN

ADNAN KHASOGGI - VICTOR LOWNES PLUS

MANY MORE HOUSEHOLD NAMES.

THE KIWI WORLD TOUR INCLUDED:

AUSTRALIA – CURACAO - EIRE - FRANCE - GERMANY

ITALY - CYPRUS - SWEDEN - DENMARK - PORTUGAL

SPAIN - BRAZIL - MOROCCO - SRI LANKA

SOUTH AFRICA - JORDAN - ISRAEL - MADEIRA

INDIA/GOA - THAILAND - VIETNAM - SINGAPORE

PANAMA - USA - BAHAMAS - CANADA - GIBRALTAR

PHILIPPINES - HONG KONG - CHINA - CUBA

BERMUDA - HAWAII - HOLLAND - SWITZERLAND